PRAISE FOR
HE'S STILL ON THE THRONE

No one has helped me learn to fear, trust and love God more than Stuart Briscoe. And in this book he gets it right once again. He does not begin with human frailty and fears and then bring a touch of God to us. Rather, he begins with the majesty and grace of God (*He Is Still on the Throne!*) and calls us to draw near to Him. In this, true faith is born and enlivened. Thank you, Stuart!

—Scott Arbeiter
President, World Relief

One thing that all of us can count on in this life is suffering—but, thankfully, we can also rely on the unchanging truth that God has not abdicated His throne. With his thorough and encouraging examination of First Peter, Stuart Briscoe reminds us that we serve a loving God who is more than able to see us through life's storms.

—Jim Daly
President, Focus on the Family

To Jill

HE'S STILL ON THE THRONE

FINDING HOPE IN A WORLD OF TROUBLE

God Bless you

HE'S STILL ON THE THRONE

FINDING HOPE IN A WORLD OF TROUBLE

STUART BRISCOE

CLC PUBLICATIONS

Fort Washington, PA 19034

He's Still on the Throne
Published by CLC Publications

U.S.A.
P.O. Box 1449, Fort Washington, PA 19034

UNITED KINGDOM
CLC International (UK)
Unit 5, Glendale Avenue, Sandycroft, Flintshire, CH5 2QP

Printed in the United States of America

ISBN (paperback): 978-1-61958-245-3
ISBN (e-book): 978-1-61958-246-0

Italics in Scripture quotations are the emphasis of the author.

Cover design by Mitch Bolton.

CONTENTS

INTRODUCTION

Bearded, bedraggled men bearing signs proclaiming, "The end is near" have long been the subject of cartoonists. The vultures, often perched on top of the signs, might add an ominous melancholy and foreboding to these scenes but the messenger and message only invite ridicule and derision. People laugh and scoff. They dismiss the warning, and go on their way. But nowadays, while many of the scoffers may not accept "the end" in a biblical sense, they are certainly uneasy about trends and less than confident about the future.

A majority of people polled in the United States think the nation is on the wrong track. I have also sensed feelings of disaffection in other parts of the world, particularly in many countries in Europe. Economists tell young people that they will be the first generation that will have to settle for a lower standard of living than enjoyed by their parents. Social mores are in a tail spin. Politicians preside over deadlock, their supporters vilifying their opponents with vitriol. The Middle East is on fire. Russia is flexing her muscles. Iran and North Korea are pursuing nuclear weaponry. Violence rules in the inner cites. Drug addiction is reaching epic proportions. Migrant populations are on the march. Many followers of Jesus are experiencing the same sense of unease or dread as the general population. Some are in danger of giving way to despair and fear and many are looking for a clear statement of encouragement and assurance as they face uncertain times.

Peter wrote his first epistle about his own difficult and dangerous days. Days he rightly suspected would get more difficult and no less perilous. His intent in writing to the small churches scattered throughout the inhospitable regions of Asia Minor was to warn the believers of their impending difficulties, to affirm them in their spiritual position and to encourage them practically to live like Christians in invidious circumstances.

Sulpicius Severus, the Roman historian, tells us that Peter was crucified during the reign of Nero, after a fire that destroyed half the city of Rome. The emperor, whose unpopularity had been well earned, was widely suspected of arson but managed to divert suspicion to the Christians who were easy prey for his malicious slander. They were horribly persecuted even to the extent that "new kinds of death were invented" as they were "devoured by dogs" and some were "set apart . . . that when the day came to a close, they should be consumed to serve for light." Eventually, it was decreed by Rome that it was "unlawful to be a Christian." ("Excerpts from Sulpicious Severus," Bk. II Chapter XXIX <PreteristCentral.com>) How much of this persecution was foreseen by Peter before he was consumed by it? We have no way of knowing; but it would appear that he was well aware that life in Rome was hard for disciples of Jesus and would probably become equally challenging for believers scattered throughout the provinces.

Peter addressed this catalogue of dire circumstances that was confronting his contemporaries in a surprisingly forthright manner. He writes, "Dear friends do not be surprised at the painful trial you are suffering, as though something strange were happening to you" (1 Pet. 4:12). Peter acknowledges that their lot is painful but does not regard it as unusual as he links their earthly sufferings to those of Christ. He characterizes these trials as something that can lead to rejoicing and ultimately to being overjoyed. There is no doubt that this kind of thinking and talking challenges the mind-set of modern followers of Jesus. We may be tempted to take a detour around Peter's writings. But this would be as sad as it would be unwise. For Peter, who knew suffering firsthand, who had battled through his own periods of uncertainty and doubt, who had known paralyzing fear and abject failure, wrote (under the promptings of the Holy Spirit) not only from personal experience but also from a keen grasp of the teachings of Jesus—teaching he heard firsthand and meditated upon and taught for approximately thirty years. There is maturity and reality in his words.

While many believers have been mercifully spared the pain and suffering of their brothers and sisters in other parts of the world, scripture does not hesitate to teach that suffering is an integral part of Christian stewardship and discipleship. Because of this, we need to be well versed on the subject, not only for our own wellbeing but also in order to rightly relate to what is happening in the church worldwide.

But even if some of us have been spared much of the physical pain that other brothers and sisters bear on a daily basis and we have never been subjected to the harsh treatment meted out to Jesus' followers living in widely different cultural situations from ours, there is much pain—emotional, psychological, relational—that is all too familiar and Peter's words speak to this just as clearly. No one is guaranteed immunity from worries about trends and many individuals experience forebodings of the future and suffer from uncertainty concerning the purposes of God. Peter has much to say on all these topics and does so not only in a blunt and forthright manner but with the encouraging heart of a shepherd of God's flock and the resolution of a convinced disciple of the risen Lord.

His words are not giddily triumphalist nor are they morbidly defeatist. Perhaps one could say he writes with a consciousness that God is still on the throne but his people are still on the earth. That the God of all grace is working from the throne toward the eternal glory of the "called" is certainly reassuring but the fact that He has intentionally left His people on the earth where His Son experienced its hostility is puzzling for some and discouraging for many who are feeling the pain. But Peter does not duck the issues of suffering neither does he offer simplistic answers to its mysteries. He says enough to strengthen the weak, encourage the timid, support the fainting, challenge the defeated and "nerve the faint endeavors" of God's people. The closing benediction of the epistle speaks volumes: "And the God of all grace, who called you to his eternal glory in Christ, after you have suffered a little while, will himself restore you and make you strong, firm and steadfast." And then he adds, "I have written to you briefly, encouraging you and testifying that this is the true grace of God. STAND FAST IN IT" (1 Pet. 5:10, 12).

1

HARD TIMES
1 Peter 1:1–2

Peter, an apostle of Jesus Christ, to God's elect, strangers in the world, scattered throughout Pontus, Galatia, Cappadocia, Asia and Bithynia, who have been chosen according to the fore-knowledge of God the Father, through the sanctifying work of the Spirit, for obedience to Jesus Christ and sprinkling by his blood: Grace and peace be yours in abundance.

1 Peter 1:1, 2

The positive tone of Peter's letter is evident in the opening words of customary introduction. Identifying himself, he promptly reminded his readers of the remarkable fact that Jesus had taken an unstable Galilean fisherman, made him into a rock and sent him into the world on a mission—to be an integral part of the church Jesus was going to build. To claim the title of apostle was to claim a special relationship with Christ. The word *apostle* is simply an Anglicization of the Greek word *apostolos* which means "a person sent with full authority." Peter was not at all bashful in this claim and it is apparent that the primitive church had no difficulty in accepting that he did indeed speak with authority in the name of Christ. The writer of the letter is immediately worth listening to because (1) his changed life gives him credibility, (2) his conviction concerning Jesus being Christ exudes authenticity and (3) his apostolic office brings a touch of authority to all he had to say.

We use the name "Jesus Christ" almost as if Jesus was our Lord's Christian name and Christ, His family name. However, we must remember that Jesus means "Savior," and "Christ" was the title that only God's chosen and anointed servant could rightly use. False messiahs have come and gone but for Peter, Jesus of Nazareth was the One whom God had sent as His anointed Redeemer.

The recipients of the letter lived in a far flung region of the Roman Empire covering the area now part of modern Turkey. How the churches in these regions were established we do not know for certain except that Paul and his companions certainly traveled in the area preaching and teaching. Also, people from these provinces were among the crowds on the Day of Pentecost. They heard Peter preach and, presumably, some of them believed and returned home with the message of Christ.

There is no doubt that life was not easy in those days, particularly for Christians living under Roman domination. But Peter spoke of his readers in glowing terms; as if to take their minds off their troubles and place them firmly on their privileges. "God's elect, strangers in the world," he called them. In the Old Testament Jehovah chose a people for Himself through whom He would make Himself and His purposes for mankind known. He called them "my people, my chosen [ones], the people I formed for myself" (Isa. 43:20–21). Peter applied similar terms to believers in his day with the intention of reminding them that, as the children of Israel were called to be God's elite corps, so they, in the midst of their problems, were similarly God's elect. It was through them that God intended to continue His redemptive work.

Years ago, when I was a member of the Royal Marines, I marveled at the way tired and dispirited troops could be raised to new heights of endeavor and involvement by the simple and expedient reminder that we belonged to an elite corps, were part of a remarkable heritage, and there were expectations which rested upon us because we wore the same uniform as those who had gone before.

Peter went on to describe his readers as "strangers in the world." He was emphasizing something painfully familiar to them: their profession of Christ put them at odds with the surrounding society.

The popular games in Rome had become so violent and cruel that Christians felt compelled to disassociate themselves from such forms of entertainment. They also declined to engage in the worship activities that involved the plethora of Roman gods. The Christian stance in these matters was deeply resented. Being against the national sport back then, as now, was not conducive to popularity. Taking a stand against the national religion was even less accepted. The fact that this religion was bound to concepts of nationalism meant that those who were against the national religion were often regarded as being, in some way, against the state. Pity the people in any society who take unpopular stands on three of the most volatile issues—sports, politics and religion!

The first Christians were regarded as oddities who would eventually go away. But as time went on, and they persisted, benign neglect turned to virulent opposition and believers, at best, were ostracized and, at worst, liquidated. When Peter called them the "scattered" people he was using a word which contained several nuances of meaning. It referred to the unfortunate circumstances of sheep being scattered or of chaff being blown by the winds. There's no doubt that the scattered believers of the early church often felt like lost sheep and windblown chaff. But seed is also scattered with very positive, fruitful results. Christians soon learned that the unpleasantness of being scattered could lead to most fruitful results if they looked at their situation as being a strategic planting by the hand of God. Again, the idea of privilege in the affairs of the Most High comes through most clearly.

Human beings have an understandable tendency to see things from an entirely human perspective. While it is understandable, it must be seen as a distorted perspective. Peter, who had done more than his share of looking at things from his own vantage point, and on one particularly painful occasion had been roundly rebuked for it, learned the hard way to see things from a divine angle. This comes through powerfully as he reminds his readers of the work of God in their lives. It is particularly noteworthy that Peter specifically outlined the work of each member of the Trinity— the Father, Son and Holy Spirit—in our salvation. Because great emphasis is often and rightly placed on the necessity for personal decision, it is not uncommon for people to view their salvation as basically dependent on that decision. But given how frail and fickle humans are, if salvation is dependent on human ability, spiritual experience would lack stability and assurance. Scripture insists that our salvation is primarily dependent on the initiative and decision of God, both of which precede any actions of man. Peter emphasized this with the words "chosen according to the foreknowledge of God the Father." God's foreknowledge or *prognosis* (the Greek word) is the basis of His choice.

Anyone who has had dealings with a physician knows something about diagnosis and prognosis. Once we are made aware of a problem, we usually want to know what the doctor believes will happen. He will probably give his opinion (or prognosis) which will be an educated guess based on experience and statistics. But even he knows how wrong he might be.

That said, the prognosis of God is different. It is not a guess and does not depend on the statistical analysis of what has previously happened. His foreknowledge is based on what He has determined to do, and nothing will stop Him or His plan. He has freely determined to offer salvation to the ungodly; freely determined to make it available through His Son; freely determined that through faith in Him and His work on the cross redemption would be available; and freely decided that those who put their faith in Christ would have eternal life, reigning with Him forever. Not one ounce of pressure was brought to bear on the Father in any of these decisions. They were all His, and He is totally committed to making sure that things work out the way He decided. These decisions, you will note, do not discount human accountability or cancel human choice. For God has also freely chosen to require human cooperation in His salvation plan as surely as He decided in the first place to make salvation available. The great benefit of this aspect of truth to those for whom the going is tough is the realization that in the final analysis, our salvation is not dependent solely on us but rather is based solidly on the immutable purposes of the Sovereign Lord. Therein lies great security for troubled believers.

The Holy Spirit, as Peter pointed out, also plays a massive role in our salvation particularly in His "sanctifying work." *Sanctify* is a word used very little today but is related to holy and saint in New Testament usage. It means to set apart. Buildings, people, vessels, animals are all said to be sanctified which means that they have a specific function for which they are suited and to which they are committed. Believers are to understand that when the Holy Spirit enters our lives at regeneration we are immediately "set apart" in that we now possess His special presence and are specially possessed by Him for His purposes. This can be called initial sanctification. However, we must not forget the continual sanctification that Scripture teaches. Once set apart for Him, the believer needs to recognize the necessity of behaving differently. In fact, behaving in a manner that is compatible with the new standing is the result of the continual "sanctifying work" of the Spirit. The end of this ongoing experience comes when finally, in the risen Lord's presence, we see Him and become like Him. But until then, the sanctifying work goes on.

When I was enlisted in the Royal Marines at the age of eighteen, I was immediately "set apart" as a member of an elite military corps. Yet, it soon became clear that I was not used to the peculiar pressures that such a position entailed. But as time went on, and through vigorous training and discipline by people skilled in such matters, I began to exhibit the poise and command expected of someone wearing the uniform. There were certainly times when I wondered if I would ever make it. Just like the "set apart" Christian, I had to realize that my position was not dependent on my performance. My position was secure. There was no way out for me! This understanding powerfully motivated me to perform appropriately.

The work of the Son is presented as "sprinkling by his blood." The Old Testament imagery contained in this expression is related to the sacrificial system where the life of the substitutionary victim was forfeited so that sin might be forgiven and judgment averted. It is significant that, at Passover, the blood of the sacrifice was collected and applied to the doorposts or to the extremities of the high priest's body, because this demonstrated that formal observation of a sacrificial act was not enough. There had to be a personal application of the merits of the sacrifice.

So it is with the believer who must have an intimate experience of forgiveness and a deeply personal knowledge of reconciliation on the basis of Christ's sacrifice. This knowledge fits the believer for a life of special relationship to the Lord—a life based on loving obedience. Peter's phrase that we are "chosen . . . for obedience" should not be overlooked, particularly when situations are dire and decisions are fraught with tension. There may have been times when early Christians living under pressure in Rome found disobedience much less physically painful than obedience, and submission to Rome much more amenable than obedience to Christ. But knowing they were called to obedience right from the outset of their spiritual experience, they likely recognized that their commitment to obedience was all part of their sprinkling through His blood. In those frightening days, they not only needed the soul anchor that only their knowledgeable experience of Christ could give them, but also a practical endowment of the "grace and peace" which the formal traditional introduction to the letter wished them. They would need peace in the midst of political and societal turmoil and grace to handle the overwhelming pressures they would be subjected to in the near future, if Peter's prediction of a "painful trial" (1 Pet. 4:12) proved correct.

There are many counselors and resources available to those who are experiencing hard times, but in the long run, only the truth of God found in Scripture can equip people for difficult times. Only the eternal Word provides the context in which temporal problems can be understood, and only the eternal Lord can supply the remedies human problems demand.

2

A POSITIVE ATTITUDE

1 Peter 1:3–5

I've never heard of a seminar on the development of bad attitudes, but I've seen many seminars on how to develop good attitudes. Now I wonder why that is. Perhaps it's because we have a natural tendency toward bad attitudes, aided by the circumstances in which we live, the environment in which we have been raised, and the situations that we are required to confront. Therefore, it is necessary for us to develop good attitudes because they don't just happen. Before developing them though, there must be the desire for a good attitude because in some situations, we develop attitudes that are so bad we have no desire to change.

Do you remember the story of the man who was lying by the pool of Bethesda? He had been disabled for thirty-eight years. The Lord Jesus went up to him and asked, "Do you want to get well?" (see John 5:6). The question appears strange because we would assume that his sole objective in lying by the pool was to be healed. It is possible, however, that the Lord Jesus asked the question because He knew that the man had an attitudinal problem. He had probably come to the point of despair, and the Lord recognized that there was nothing He could do for him if the man really didn't desire to be made whole.

Quite often we give up because of difficult circumstances. We quit because of the complexity of a situation or because of the apparent absence of solutions. We stop trying to rectify anything and just allow all our circumstances to overwhelm us, our situations to take control of us and our natural tendencies to pull us down. But somewhere along the line we need to get around to desiring to be different. How does that come about?

Developing a Positive Attitude

Believers develop positive attitudes by, first, having a solid grasp of divine truth—the revealed Word of God in their hearts. For example, notice how the Apostle Peter, referring to God's work in our lives, says, "In his great mercy he has given us new birth into a living hope through the resurrection of Jesus Christ from the dead" (1:3). The thought of a living hope seems to spring to Peter's mind as soon as he starts writing.

The Scriptures teach that, by nature, we are dead to God. The only thing that is of any help to dead people is new life. God, recognizing our spiritual deadness, made it possible for Christ to die and rise again for us. He promised that this risen Lord Jesus would be made available to us in the person of the Holy Spirit and that He would come into our lives and spark newness of life within us. In fact, it would be just like being "born again"—born from above. This is probably the earliest occasion the expression "born again" is used in Scripture. The well known reference in John 3 would be written at least thirty years after Peter's epistle. It is unfortunate that many people spend so much time arguing about the born-again experience. They want to know the when and the how without realizing that the reality of being born again is shown not by the careful rehearsing of details surrounding the experience but by the clear evidence of a new life. People don't come to me and question whether I was born on the basis of my recollections of my original birthday. They appear to accept the fact of my birth because of the reality of my life. The important thing about being born again is that we are living anew in the very same way. Just as the important thing about being born is that we are alive! God has moved into our lives in remarkable fashion and He has infused us with newness of life, making us a new creation. We will never be the same again. It is a gift we didn't deserve, we can never earn and can never pay off. It is something that God freely decided to give to human beings who were lost in sin and at enmity with God. Out of His great mercy, He gave us newness of life.

They tell us that "hope springs eternal in the human breast!" I don't know about the "eternal" but I do know that people demonstrate a determined need for something to hope for. Every four years, we elect a new president, pinning all our hopes upon him or her only to be disappointed repeatedly. But we are determined to try again! Believers have a hope that refuses to be dashed. It is a hope that is overwhelmingly confident. It is something that God has built into our lives and is rooted in the fact that, having been given Christ, we can be sure God will give us all things that we need. Romans 8:32 asks, "He who did not spare his own Son, but gave him up for us all—how will he not also, along with him, graciously give us all things?" Paul's question is rhetorical. No answer is necessary because the answer is obvious. If He gave us Christ to die for us and to live within us, and we're born again through His indwelling presence, how can we possibly imagine that God wouldn't give us everything we need, along with Christ, for time and eternity!? When we understand this, there is hope. But it's not hope in humanity; it's hope in deity.

Peter goes a step further as he reminds us that, "he has given us new birth into a living hope through the resurrection of Jesus Christ from the dead" (1:3). Why do we pin our hopes on God doing something certain and sure for us? The answer is because of "the resurrection." There is an air of solid certainty about the believer's hope. I like to look at it this way: I have problems. I look at them, try to understand them, evaluate them and then quickly remind myself that God also had a problem. His problem was that His Son, whom He ordained as King of Kings and Lord of Lords, was, unfortunately, dead. However, God addressed the problem in superlative fashion.

He raised Jesus from the dead. So now, whenever we confront problems, we are able to relate them to God's simple and dramatic solution of His own problem and say, "God, You are the God of my problems as well as my successes. You are the God of my beginning, my end and everything in between. This means that I can relate this problem to You. Knowing the magnitude of what You do with problems, I am confident You can handle this one." The believer's hope is born of confidence and based on the historical fact that God raised Christ from the dead!

Peter's positive approach to life is also related to his understanding of the gift of our new status. He shares that not only have we been born again into a living hope but we've also been born again into "an inheritance," and that means that we have become "heirs of God and co-heirs with Christ" (Rom. 8:17).

It is highly probable that the words Peter heard from the Master's lips in Galilee were echoing in his heart: "Do not store up for yourselves treasures on earth, where moth and rust destroy, and where thieves break in and steal. But store up for yourselves treasures in heaven, where moth and rust do not destroy, and where thieves do not break in and steal" (Matt. 6:19–20). Then our Lord added these pungent words: "For where your treasure is, there your heart will be also" (6:21). Perhaps Peter was thinking of the change in his own perspective—from a life absorbed with fishing nets, a leaky old boat, some stinky fish and the salt to pack them in, to a life of bigger and grander and greater things. God had given him the insight into what it meant to be a son of God, an heir of God, an eternal creature. He had given him a vista of heaven and a sense of spiritual values.

Some preachers delight in sermons that have three points—preferably alliterative! In Peter, they find a kindred spirit, for he described the inheritance as follows: *aphthartos* or incorruptible, *amiantos* or undefiled, and *amarantos* or unfading (see 1 Pet. 1:4). He is simply taking what Jesus said in the Sermon on the Mount about moth, rust and thieves and showing the security and certainty of the inheritance because it is "kept in heaven." The strength of the word *kept* is apparent when we remember that *keep* can also mean the part of a castle where people under attack could run for survival. In the keep, they were literally kept!

It's amazing how good of an attitude believers can have when they understand their status and the unassailable security of the inheritance to which they are entitled. Added to this is the gift of a new security which Peter describes as follows: "Who through faith are shielded by God's power until the coming of the salvation that is ready to be revealed in the last time" (1:5). There are three tenses of salvation. It is possible for a person to say, "I have been saved." It is equally necessary for a person to say, "I am being saved" and in addition, to predict, "I will be saved." These statements appear to be contradictory unless we realize we are saved from different things. When we say "I have been saved," we mean we have been saved from sin's penalty. We have been forgiven. Our sin has been reckoned to Christ, Christ's righteousness has been reckoned to us, and we can look the world in the eye and say, "Folks, take a good, long, hard look. There is a saved sinner standing in front of you."

Many believers have a problem with the power of their sinful nature. Yet God graciously makes it possible for us to overcome that old power of sin within us so that we can, on a daily basis say, "I am being saved progressively." There are things in my life that don't exist to the same extent that they may have twelve months ago. That's growth, that's maturity, that's development and that's progress! All of this can be explained by the fact that we are being saved through the power of the Spirit from our sin and its consequences. In a healthy spiritual experience, we should be sensing that from the moment we have been saved, we are being saved.

Peter adds that we are, through faith, "shielded by God's power unto the coming of the salvation that is ready to be revealed in the last time" (1:5). He is talking about ultimately being saved from sin's presence. In "the last time" the Lord Jesus will come and take His people to be with Him, and the heavens and earth will dissolve with fervent heat, as Peter states in his second epistle. Then we'll say, "Praise God you have saved me from sin's penalty, you did go on saving me from sin's power and now the whole thing is finished. You have saved me from sin's presence and I live in a realm where righteousness and justice dwells."

Now think on this for a minute. If God has already said we have been saved so that, progressively, we might grow more and more like the Lord Jesus, and He knows that this progression will find its completion when Christ comes again and saves us from sin's presence, isn't it reasonable to assume that if God started it, He will finish it? If salvation means anything, it means salvation in its entirety from the penalty, power and presence of sin. So if He started it, we can be confident that He will continue it and complete it. Therein lies our security. Now notice we are "shielded by God's power" (1:5). Having already linked our hope to the resurrection, Peter links our security to the power of God, demonstrated in such undeniable and exhilarating fashion in that same event. Believers, often fearful of our situations when under pressure, need look only to the resurrection for assurance that God's power is adequate in all cases. However, the power is only operative in our lives "through faith," which means you have to believe it to enjoy it. It may be a surprise to realize that the way to produce a good attitude in people is to teach them truth. Teaching, of course, encourages learning, and learning only happens as we continuously study and apply the lessons. If we don't, we will come under the gravitational pull of everything around us and in no time be down again.

It is also vital that we have constant reminders of the truth and continual encouragement to apply the truth we know. When the truth is ever-present, we will have no problem seeing that the church of Jesus Christ must be a community where there is a solid diet of the teaching of the Word of God, a community in which interpersonal relationships are developed so that we can encourage each other and a community in which we have such loving communication with people that they are able to remind us when we're "off the wall." They will be empowered to correct us, turn us around and help us to build the positive attitudes that are so necessary. Our society today is riddled with bad attitudes on every hand—suspicion, distrust, deceit, abuse, selfishness, egocentricity and latent violence are all present. In the church of Jesus Christ, we need to get our theology squared away and encourage each other to apply it so that we can begin to have some good, solid, healthy attitudes, in stark contrast to the world around us.

Demonstrating a Positive Attitude

Peter suspects he may not have long until his head is separated from the rest of him, or he is crucified upside down.

Yet you would never guess it from his buoyant words: "Praise be to the God and Father of our Lord Jesus Christ!" (1:3). A positive attitude is often demonstrated by praise. In Peter's case, his objective in recounting these truths with which his readers are familiar is to get them to join him in that praise. He asserts that we should praise because, in His great mercy, God gave us a new birth, a living hope and an inheritance. We should praise Him because that inheritance doesn't perish, never spoils, is never corrupted and is reserved in heaven for us. We should also praise Him because He has given us His own power to shield us, and will complete the salvation He started in us. When our enemies have done their worst, which could possibly mean death, it will also mean an early introduction to our eternal inheritance. Praiseworthy indeed!

Unfortunately there is a tendency for believers to become absorbed with our hard circumstances when things get tough. We spend too much time and effort searching for a quick solution instead of relating to our most profound beliefs. It's in these moments that we must center our hearts and minds on who God is, what He has done, what He is doing, and particularly, on what He is going to do. Praise has to be intelligently rooted in truth rather than floated on our feelings.

It worries me when I hear some well meaning but insensitive person slapping a troubled believer on the back and exhorting them to, "Praise the Lord!" People going through deep waters don't need back slaps. They need someone to get in the deep water with them and to quietly and gently remind them of the deep truths of the faith—preferably when they are ready to be encouraged. You'll notice that Peter, despite his difficulties, uses the word *hope*. Believers, in addition to being praising people, should be filled with an expectant hope. He also shows us that Christians should have an exuberant faith because we're "shielded by God's power" through our faith. Praise, hope and faith are the stuff that makes a positive attitude and the means whereby it is exhibited (see 1:5).

Our society may not realize it but the world needs to see a church that is producing people with positive attitudes because, quite frankly, anybody can be negative, anybody can be destructive and anybody can be divisive. It takes very a different kind of people to live positively in a negative environment.

One evening after there had been a lot of negative criticism of a reasonable and well-thought-out ministry proposal at our church board meeting, the chairman said very quietly, "It's a well-established fact that any jackass can kick down a barn but it takes a craftsman to build one." Then he added, "Are there any craftsmen?" The silence was deafening for a few seconds until the room exploded in rueful laughter! Attitudes were checked, apologies offered and accepted and a fresh cooperative spirit moved in. That's how it should be! So in turn, my question to every believer is this: "Are there any craftsmen?" You can tell them by their attitudes.

3

JOY-FILLED LIVING
1 Peter 1:6–9

The American Declaration of Independence states that human beings have the inalienable right to life, liberty and the pursuit of happiness. There is little doubt that considerable time and energy have been spent both at government and individual levels in an attempt to ensure the happiness of the people. In fact, I'm not sure that anyone can doubt that great strides have been made in reducing poverty, curing endemic illnesses, combating crime, improving housing, guaranteeing civil rights and a thousand other things that certainly have made life easier for many people. But none of this has produced wholesale happiness. This is one of the great puzzles confronting social engineers, politicians, think tanks and public-spirited billionaires.

Part of the problem is that human happiness too often depends on happenings. If the happenings don't happen the way we want our happenings to happen, we are unhappy. There is, therefore, a great emphasis on controlling situations, solving problems and manipulating circumstances with the intention of making sure that all the happenings happen the way we want them to happen—and then we will be happy. In reality, this is a fantasy wrapped in futility because so many of these happenings are clearly beyond our control and relentlessly resist our interventions. Moreover, if it was possible to organize happenings so they happen the way we want them to happen, boredom—not happiness— would be the result!

The Bible's themes of joy in suffering and peace in conflict are both more realistic in light of the failure of our organized society to produce the ideal state wherein happiness reigns supreme. Peter's first Epistle is a marvelous illustration of the Christian experience of joy, written, as it was, against the somber background of persecution and suffering. He is writing to people who he says, "may have had to suffer grief in all kinds of trials" (1:6) and he tells his readers not to be "surprised at the painful trial" they are suffering (4:12). He also outlines his expectation that they will experience a quality of joy that can only be described as "inexpressible and glorious" (1:8).

The conventional wisdom of our day or any day would say these circumstances could only produce pain and anguish. Yet Christian truth speaks of joy that will transcend such circumstances because it is related to something infinitely more stable and secure.

Peter informs his readers that their joy will come through their faith, their hope and their love—most emphatically not through their circumstances. This is one of the most powerful lessons Christians need to learn and be reminded of, and it is one of the most powerful Christian distinctions that must be modeled before a happiness-craving society.

The Joy That Comes Through Faith

Just like the soil is important to the seed, it is the ground of faith which determines the results of faith. Great faith in an unworthy object produces despair and disaster. You can commit yourself wholeheartedly to thin ice and drown by faith. On the other hand, just a little faith on very thick ice can be as safe as standing on reinforced concrete.

Notice that Peter says, "In this you greatly rejoice" (1:6). Rejoice in what? The answer is found in the opening five verses of the letter. First, he speaks of the revelation of the Father's "mercy." God has freely chosen to treat sinful humanity with mercy. It is a divine initiative, a divine truth and a divine revelation. When we know and believe it, we rejoice!

Second, Peter points out the results of the Son's ministry, including "sprinkling by His blood" (1:2). The benefits of His death have been applied to our lives, resulting in the forgiveness of our sins and reconciliation with God. This is not an abstract theological premise. it is a spiritual reality. We live in the joyful blessings of the substitutionary death of Jesus our Lord.

Third, there is the promise of the Son's return in the verse that says, "ready to be revealed in the last time" (1:5). He will come in great glory to incorporate His people into His eternal kingdom. When we see Him, we will be like Him. Our eternal destiny is secure. In this, we rejoice!

Fourth, Peter talks about the "sanctifying work of the Spirit" (1:2). There is clear evidence of Holy Spirit's impact on believers in the changing, converting work that He has accomplished. Believers who can compare who they are now to who they were without Christ, have little difficulty being joyfully thankful for their transformation and have good reason to look to the ongoing work of the Spirit's grace in the days to come. What a cause for great joy!

Fifth, Peter refers to "the resurrection of Jesus Christ from the dead" (1:3). Death is often described as "the last enemy" (see 1 Cor. 15:26). The thought of dying can certainly fill the human heart with foreboding but the resurrection of Christ takes away death's sting, and replaces these thoughts with joyful anticipations of glory. Therefore, the ground of faith is our Heavenly Father who is totally committed to being God, knows the end from the beginning and who acts out of His eternal "foreknowledge" (1 Pet. 1:2). These are the constant factors in a world that is full of uncertainties and inconsistencies. Those who know this "greatly rejoice."

Peter goes on to talk about the growth of faith. Presumably the "little while" and the "grief" and "all kinds of trials" mentioned above refer to the time of Nero's persecution. This grief is not simply the product of a callous, cold fate but is related to the God of whom he has spoken so warmly. He sees the trials as being purposeful in the context of God's work in the believers' lives. The purpose is explained as follows: "These have come so that your faith . . . may be proved genuine and may result in praise, glory and honor when Jesus Christ is revealed" (1:7). As faith is firmly grounded, joy is established. As faith grows, joy flourishes. The merciful God allows His children to go through times of testing so their faith can grow. It is a sad fact of our humanity that when times are easy and life is pleasant, when all is well in our little corner of the world, our faith-life frequently takes a back seat. Likewise, when trouble looms, for many people, prayer grows, faith deepens and maturity occurs.

Faith is "of greater worth than gold" (1:7). The commodity everybody thinks is the most valuable, in actuality, is not. In Peter's folio, gold is far inferior to a faith that's grounded in who God is and what God is doing. He adds the thought that their faith is going to be tested so that they can really find out how valuable it is. How do we find out if faith is more valuable than gold? We may be confronted with the choice between making a fast buck at the expense of a principle related to Christian faith or standing for a particular principle at the expense of a buck. This may not seem to be a "fiery trial," but our faith might certainly be singed by it!

What about health? Is it possible that our health can be more important than faith? How will we know? One of these days we may get sick, and our reaction will show very quickly what's more important—our faith or our health. The fiery trial of poor health has destroyed the faith of some and refined the faith of others. In doing so, it has revealed the real nature of faith. We find out the value of our faith by putting it to the test, and Peter insists that God helps in the evaluation process. Not only is our faith more important than gold but the testing of our faith is more important than the refining of gold. There is a commodity called "fool's gold" which isn't gold at all. It looks like it, but it is actually an iron commodity. It is necessary to "fire" gold to find out if it is real gold or fool's gold. In the same way that there is a refining of gold, there must be a refining of faith. At the risk of mixing metaphors, there is a similarity between refining gold and sifting wheat. Scripture uses both to great effect. I wonder if Peter's mind, as he is writing, is going back to the days when the Lord Jesus said to him, "Simon, Simon, Satan has asked to sift you as wheat" (see Luke 22:31).

Even a fisherman like Simon knew how farmers on the hillside handled the harvest. They beat the harvested grain and then threw the grain up in the air so that the chaff was blown away in the wind. Satan had asked for the chance to get at the disciples and hurl them up in the air to disorient them. The Master had given permission but added, "I have prayed for you, Simon, that your faith may not fail" (22:32). Apparently the dissension among the disciples was being caused by Peter, hence Jesus singling him out for specific prayer. It was probably also common knowledge to the Christians in Asia Minor that Peter, on that awful night of the crucifixion, had denied Christ three times. Yet, despite it all, he emerged from these and other trials, held by the prayers of the Lord, a sadder but wiser man. He was saddened by his lack of faith, but wise about the limits of his faith. Peter found out that, at first, most of his faith was in himself, and that spelled disaster. He had said, "Lord, I am ready to go with you to prison and to death" (22:33) only to discover that his noble intentions were not matched by noble achievement. This was a sad but glorious discovery that only a painful trial could reveal. That night, the air may have been full of Peter's chaff but not long afterward; his real faith began to show.

Let's also consider the goal of faith as Peter writes: "These have come so that your faith . . . may be proved genuine and may result in praise, glory and honor when Jesus Christ is revealed" (1:7). He calls the goal of faith "the salvation of . . . souls" (1:9) which we are receiving, but which we also look forward to receiving. This paradoxical concept is both similar and related to the truth that the Kingdom has come but is yet to come. The Kingdom has dawned, but it has yet to reach its full noontime glory. In similar fashion, when we look at our salvation experience, we can see that we are not what we used to be but we can also admit that we are not what we ought to be. Most of all, we can rejoice that we are not fully what we will be. This thought encourages us to press on until we enjoy all that God has for us in His salvation. When everything is easy and fun, people naturally concentrate on the pleasant here and now. But when the easy becomes hard, and the fun becomes tears, and the "I am just fine" becomes rough, thought patterns changing dramatically, questions like, "Where am I heading? What's going to happen? To whom do I belong?" abound. If there is a spiritual orientation, the answers will come from the biblical truths concerning the return in glory of the risen Lord and the exciting prospects of sharing in that glory. But it is a sad truth that it sometimes requires the testing of our faith to bring us to the point of interest in the goal of our faith.

For some of us, life is just beautiful and sweet—all sunshine and butterflies. Fiery trials, Jesus coming again, heaven, the trial of faith are subjects of little interest. But those of you whose lives are full of these pleasantries must know that testing times will come. The going will get tough, so we are encouraged to learn these things now so that the Holy Spirit will bring them to our remembrance when we need them.

The Joy That Comes Through Hope

There is a great note of hope in what Peter is saying here. First, notice that hope comes through comparison. For example Peter says, "Though now for a little while you may have had to suffer grief" (1:6). When we're in the midst of suffering, a trial or temptation or difficulty, "interminable" sounds more relevant than "a little while." Is there no end to this? Is there no light at the end of the tunnel? Is there no way of easing the pain? Will I ever get over this trauma? Can I ever forgive and forget what has happened to me? The interminable present turns into "a little while" for Peter when seen in relation to "the last time" (1:5). Eyes fixed on the little while here will likely see only interminable and overwhelming difficulties. On the other hand, the unpleasant now, seen in the light of the last times, is touched with rays of hope that are as transforming as the touch of dawn on the darkness of the night. Joy is to be found in this kind of hope.

Peter speaks of the "grief" they will suffer in the same context as the "sprinkled blood" (the suffering and dying of the Lord Jesus). Some of them, including Peter and Paul, will shed their blood as martyrs. However, there will be an involuntary aspect to their deaths. This is in marked contrast to Christ laying down His life voluntarily for them. Peter can compare the little while of suffering now to the last days of all that lies ahead of him, and he can also compare the sufferings that they are going through in his present with the sufferings that Christ endured. Jeremiah, the weeping prophet, spoke prophetically of our Lord, "Look around and see. Is any suffering like my suffering?" (Lam. 1:12). The answer is no. There is no sorrow like His, no agony like His, and no passion like His. And how did His agony and His sorrow and His passion end? In a glorious resurrection. What is the end of our suffering and grief for a little while? A glorious resurrection. Therein lies hope, the seedpod of joy.

Peter goes on to compare "gold, which perishes" with an inheritance that "can never perish, spoil or fade—kept in heaven for you" (1:4). If our hope is in our gold and our investments, then we will be looking for ways to preserve it, protect it, and multiply it. We will be watching the market, monitoring the news, and interpreting events that focus on profit. We will be looking to economics for answers and to politics for solutions. This might make us astute investors, but I want to remind you of something that I heard when I was a young boy and never forgot. In England, they publish the contents of people's wills after probate. One day I heard two of my relatives speaking. One said, "Did you know that so and so's will was in the paper this morning?" The other one said, "No, how much did he leave?" And the answer was, "Everything." I remember the sheer shock of that answer! One of these days we will all leave everything. Then all that will matter will be "an inheritance that can never perish, spoil or fade—kept in heaven for you." Compare the two and hope will well up in your heart. In the testing time, hope will grip you and joy will flow like a river.

Hope also comes through a sense of completion. It's understandable that Peter speaks about the end of the age. He knows he is coming to the end of his days, and he's got a feeling that the infant church may be coming to the end of its days too. He still remembers that day on the Mount of Olives when he and others stood looking up into heaven and the angels told them, "This same Jesus, who has been taken from you into heaven, will come back in the same way you have seen him go" (Acts 1:11). The early disciples expected Him back in their lifetime, and in difficult circumstances they no doubt encouraged themselves with this thought: "Christ will be back soon to establish His glorious kingdom." Peter still remembers the awful ache in his heart when, on crucifixion night, he realized the Lord would not establish His kingdom as the disciples expected. However, the resurrection appearances changed all that and he began to understand that the Kingdom is not an earthly kingdom; that it is going to come to its climax at Christ's glorious return. So Peter's heart is full of the thought that the Lord will complete all that He started, and he looks forward to being involved in all that is going to happen.

Recently on a television show I was asked as soon as they opened the telephones, "Do you believe that Jesus is coming again soon?"

"I do not know," I replied.

"You mean to tell me that Jesus isn't coming soon?"

"No, I didn't tell you that Jesus wasn't coming soon. I just told you that I don't know when He is coming. I know He is coming. I know He is coming when He's ready. And I know He will complete all He started when He comes."

The person at the other end of the phone said, "Well, I thought you could have given me something definite on this."

So I said. "I can. His coming is nearer now than it was when we started talking, and that's definite!" We should avoid getting wrapped up in date picking because Jesus maintains that glorious element of surprise. And when He comes with the sound of the trumpet, there may also be a great laugh, and He may say, "Caught you! Here I am!" Therein lies our joy.

The Joy That Comes Through Love

Peter writes, "Though you have not seen him, you love him; and even though you do not see him now, you believe in him and are filled with an inexpressible and glorious joy" (1:8). This inexpressible and glorious joy also comes with our love for Him.

In the Garden of Gethsemane, Jesus prays in an agony of spirit while Peter is asleep. He had the great gift of sleep! He wakes up and an armed mob has come to take the Lord Jesus! Peter leaps to his feet, whips out his sword and prepares to defend his Lord against the mob. That's commitment! That's love! That's enthusiasm! Vintage Peter! The commitment of his love showed in the garden as he put his life on the line with a sword in his hand. Unfortunately, this commitment unraveled soon after. After his disastrous failure, Peter travels back to Galilee convinced he was good for nothing except catching fish. He meets the Lord by the side of the lake. The Lord Jesus makes breakfast, sits down by Peter and says, "Peter, do you love me?" Tentatively Peter responds until, under the gentle, persistent probing of the Lord, he insists passionately, "Yes, you know I love you!"

Here, Peter's love is no longer the rugged kind of love that takes men into danger to protect those they love. It is a quiet, introspective, warm appreciation of failure and forgiveness, grace and kindness. Peter's sword-in-hand love stirs the blood. His response to the Lord's forgiveness warms the heart. Truly "love is a many splendor'd thing" and when Christ is the subject and object of our love, we know it leads inexorably to the ultimate glory of sharing eternity with Him. In other words, "the goal of [our] faith" equals "the salvation of our [souls]" (1:9). the ideal state wherein happiness reigns supreme. Peter's first Epistle is a marvelous illustration of the Christian experience of joy, written, as it was, against the somber background of persecution and suffering. He is writing to people who he says, "may have had to suffer grief in all kinds of trials" (1:6) and he tells his readers not to be "surprised at the painful trial" they are suffering (4:12). He also outlines his expectation that they will experience a quality of joy that can only be described as "inexpressible and glorious" (1:8).

The conventional wisdom of our day or any day would say these circumstances could only produce pain and anguish. Yet Christian truth speaks of joy that will transcend such circumstances because it is related to something infinitely more stable and secure.

Peter informs his readers that their joy will come through their faith, their hope and their love—most emphatically not through their circumstances. This is one of the most powerful lessons Christians need to learn and be reminded of, and it is one of the most powerful Christian distinctions that must be modeled before a happiness-craving society.

4

TAKING SALVATION SERIOUSLY

1 PETER 1:10–12

The Old Testament prophets who predicted the coming of the Messiah, His sufferings and subsequent glories, didn't fully understand all they were predicting. But they were terribly interested in what was going on. They knew that God was working in their lives and saying something to their contemporaries, but they also recognized that He was speaking to succeeding generations. They recognized that God was speaking about their immediate situation but they also sensed that He was speaking about some future realities. It was clear to them that God was speaking about material things but they also knew that His words, through them, were concerned with eternal issues that had spiritual consequences. There was much they knew but much more they didn't know and, because of this, they were deeply engaged in their prophetic work. They searched "intently and with the greatest care" (1:10) to find out all they could about this message of salvation that they were prophetically predicting and presenting.

Angels are also desperately and anxiously examining the whole subject of salvation (see 1:12). The Greek word

Peter uses to describe the angels' "longing to look" is the same word that was used to describe Peter and John on Resurrection Day as they stooped down to look into the mystery of the empty tomb and the missing body. Angels are stooping down, peering into the earth, and looking into the human situation. They are fascinated with this whole subject of salvation and are trying to grasp it, trying to understand it to the full.

Peter's concern was that, while the prophets were so interested and the angels were so enthralled, too many humans appeared by comparison to lack a similar intensity. The prophets only knew a fraction of what humans in the future know, and the angels have long recognized that there is no way they can experience salvation like a human, yet, with all their limitations, both angels and prophets seemed more excited about the whole subject of salvation.

Peter was firmly convinced that the future aspect of salvation was particularly relevant in light of the immediate circumstances in which his readers were living. Let me remind you that Peter talks about salvation in three tenses. In the past tense, he said we have been sprinkled with the blood of Christ. In the present tense, he said that we are being sanctified by the Holy Spirit (see 1:2). But in the future tense, he spoke of the end of our salvation at the appearing of Jesus Christ (see 1:5). Peter expected Jesus to return soon. He realized that Nero might do something crazy and he, Peter, would likely die a martyr's death. In fact, the Lord Jesus Himself had given a very pointed clue concerning the possibility that Peter's life would be terminated by martyrdom (see John 21:18–19) So for Peter, the storm clouds were gathering and it was time to look to the end of all things and the beginning of eternity. Peter knew that his entrance into the future would be accomplished either by death or translation at Jesus Christ's appearing. Either way, to him it was clear that he and his contemporaries should be serious about their salvation.

Peter, in his defense before the Sanhedrin, stated concerning Christ, "Salvation is found in no one else, for there is no other name under heaven given to men by which we must be saved" (Acts 4:12). That's what you call an unequivocal statement, particularly to a hostile congregation. This council of men didn't want to hear it. They didn't want to hear that they had to be saved, and certainly not that they must be saved through Jesus Christ; that there was no alternative. It was this unequivocal, three dimensional, no nonsense salvation that prophets and angels found so captivating and which apostles preached so fervently. It is this salvation that believers today cannot afford to ignore or to treat casually.

The Curse of Casualness

Sometimes casualness is demonstrated by disbelief. Disbelief is particularly popular in a world where we are blessed scientifically. Scientists have discovered that we are very closely related to the animal kingdom. Because they know our marked similarities, they can experiment on animals to learn about human physical and emotional makeup. Unfortunately, this type of beneficial research has led some influential people to conclude that humans are really only sophisticated animals. I often wonder if that is an insult to animals! Seriously though, from a biblical point of view, we cannot accept that we are just sophisticated animals because we are spiritual beings of eternal consequence. That is why Peter emphasizes the salvation of our souls. He is interested in our eternal destiny. He is concerned about our unique human spirituality.

The conflict between scientifically induced theories and biblical principles has led many people to decide for science and to disbelieve the Bible. This has led to total casualness regarding the message of salvation. This is the environment in which many of us spend our days. Therefore, it is no surprise that disbelief and its attendant, casualness, abound. Others don't disbelieve; they are simply disinterested. They say, "Sure, I believe. I'm a person of eternal significance. Of course there is a God, but frankly I'm not interested. There are far more important things in life for me. When I get old, when I've had my fling, I'll be interested." This casualness is somewhat unnerving, particularly when compared to the prophets who knew only a fraction of what we know and yet were enraptured. The angels who can't experience what we have been offered are leaning out of heaven on tiptoe, excited to see salvation at work on earth.

Then there are those who demonstrate their casualness by complete disdain. While at a dinner party one evening with a number of surgeons, I heard one of them say to a well-known colleague, "You amaze me. When it comes to medicine you're brilliant. When it comes to surgery you're superb. But then you sacrifice it all for this Christianity nonsense. I don't understand you."

I said to him, "I don't understand you. As a scientist, you express a total disdain for well-documented areas of human experience without being willing even to consider their validity or experiment in the area of the spiritual. Your casual approach amazes me!"

Institutions suffer from the sheer curse of casualness too. Educational institutions are frequently casual about moral values, eternal issues and spiritual realities. People in these institutions would prefer to root us exclusively in the material, the temporal and the animalistic. They would have us believe that we happened accidentally and are drifting, inexorably, towards extinction. Yet, even more worrisome, the church in many instances has become casual about the salvation of people's souls and about their eternal well being.

Years ago, Jill and I were invited to go to the International Congress on World Evangelism in Lausanne, Switzerland. Another ecclesiastical conference was going on at the same time in nearby Geneva. At the Congress, I spoke to a reporter from one of the Washington newspapers. He said, "You need an ambassador doing Kissinger-style shuttle diplomacy between Lausanne and Geneva. He should help the church decide whether human beings are eternally valid. Many of those guys in Geneva don't believe that there is such a thing as hell. They believe basically in the here and now, so they concentrate on material things, on earthly considerations. But you guys up here believe that people have souls. You believe in heaven, hell and salvation. So of course you are concerned about the eternal destiny of people. The Christian church must decide what she believes. Do people have souls? Do they have eternal consequence? Is there a heaven? Is there a hell? Is there sin? Is there forgiveness? Is the cross meaningful? Is there salvation or isn't there? Because if there is, get your act together and get serious. And if there isn't, put up the shutters and become a social agency."

It was a sad day for our world when it became necessary to ask the church whether she really believed in the necessity of salvation. But the words of the Washington reporter need to be repeated! The curse of casualness is a compounded curse when it appears in the church.

The curse of casualness comes over in disbelief, in disdain, in disinterest and will produce distance from God. It robs people of reality and life, and banishes them to what I call, lost-ness.

The Strength of Seriousness

We take our salvation seriously because we have a sense of privilege. In comparison to the prophets, we know so much. Compared to the angels, our experience of forgiveness and reconciliation is so great.

Simeon was a godly man, a holy man waiting for the "consolation of Israel" (Luke 2:25). He was waiting for the arrival of Messiah. It had been revealed to him, as he spent hours and hours trying to understand the Scriptures, that not only would the Messiah come, but he, Simeon, would not die until He came. One day, a young couple brought their little boy to be circumcised. Simeon was on duty that day and as he looked at the little boy his face lit up. He lifted his head to heaven and said, "Now dismiss your servant in peace. For my eyes have seen your salvation" (Luke 2:29–30). All his life he'd searched diligently to know what salvation was and, just at the end of his days (he was a very old man), he discovered that salvation was in Jesus Christ. Many people have known this truth since they've known anything, but Simeon didn't. What a privilege we have compared to Simeon!

John the Baptist was second to none among the prophets, according to Jesus. He spent his time preaching, "Prepare the way for the Lord, make straight paths for him" (Matt. 3:3). People would come to him and say, "Are you the one who shall come?" He responded with "No, no, I'm not the one who should come. He will come after me, but He is preferred before me. I'm not even fit to polish His shoes" (see Luke 3). But then he got thrown in prison and had second thoughts. He sent a message inquiring whether Jesus really was Messiah. John the Baptist didn't have the fullness of truth we have, yet he preached with such intensity that, to silence him, they threw him in jail. Such intensity is remarkable when compared to the relative disinterest shown by those of us who know far more today.

Angels know about the holiness of God in a way that we don't. Their knowledge of the judgment of God, the majesty of God and the sheer power of God is unique. But they don't know what it is like to be saved. They have never been saved. They are servants, not sons. They have never known what it is to be so loved that the only Son of God would die on a cross for them. But we do! The angels have vast stores of knowledge and experience but, compared to ours, their knowledge has severe limitations. To look at the angels in this way is to sense our special place of privilege.

My dad was trying to explain salvation to a friend of his, but nothing seemed to make sense. Finally the frustrated friend looked at my dad and said, "Stan, I guess this salvation thing is a bit like falling in love. It's better felt than telt." That was his funny way of getting told to rhyme. The angels have "telt" it for centuries but never "felt" it for a second.

Salvation should be taken seriously because there is a great sense of authenticity about it. Peter introduces the Holy Spirit in these verses. He says the prophets were "trying to find out the time and the circumstances to which the Spirit of Christ in them was pointing" (1:11). He adds a comment about those who "preached the gospel to you by the Holy Spirit sent from heaven" (1:12). He speaks of the ministry of the Holy Spirit both in the prophets and through the preachers. Peter is referring, of course, to the inspiration of Scripture.

In his second epistle, he goes on to talk about it again, explaining that the prophets didn't dream up the things they said but spoke and wrote "as they were carried along by the Holy Spirit" (2 Pet. 1:21). Peter's word to describe the inspirational work of the Holy Spirit is the word that also describes the wind getting into the sail of the sailboat, filling it full and sweeping it along. A perfect description as that's exactly what happened to the prophets.

It's one thing to look at our Bible and say it's just an old dusty, dry book about a bunch of people who lived in the Middle East thousands of years ago and ask, "Who cares?" The answer will be "Nobody cares!" But if we believe that the Word of God was inspired by the Holy Spirit, as the prophets were moved by the Spirit, then we must believe that the Bible is a document of eternal significance and the message of salvation has authenticity. That Peter believed this with all his heart is evident from his preaching. When he found himself in situations, he related them to what the prophets had said. On the day of Pentecost, the believers were all jumping around and dancing, filled with the Holy Spirit. And the onlookers, understandably, thought they were drunk. But Peter jumped up and said, "These men are not drunk, as you suppose . . . this is what was spoken by the prophet Joel!" (Acts 2:15–16).

Peter saw the authenticity of the inspired prophetic message. When he was required to make his defense in front of authorities, he spoke from the Old Testament. He talked about Jesus' resurrection and insisted the Old Testament predicted it. He shared with them how David, the great psalmist, king and prophet, wrote, "You will not abandon me to the grave, nor will you let your Holy One see decay" (Ps. 16:10; Acts 2:27). "Do you think David is talking about himself?" Peter asked his hearers. "Of course not. You know where his tomb is. You know he is dead and buried. Open his tomb; his body is corrupt. He's not talking about himself. He was a prophet and knew that God had promised him on oath that he would place one of his descendants on his throne. Seeing what was ahead, he spoke of the resurrection of Christ" (see Acts 2:30–31). What an authentic word we have in Scripture! When we acknowledge our privilege and accept the Bible's authenticity, we will become serious about both salvation and scripture.

Peter said that the Spirit preached through the preachers who were responsible for founding the churches of Asia Minor. They were not desperate refugees who came along and told fantasy stories. They were people inspired by the Holy Spirit. And as they spoke, there was an authenticity about them and their message. The combination of Spirit-inspired Word, Spirit-anointed preaching, Spirit-aided hearing and Spirit-prompted response produces an authentic experience of God that must be taken seriously.

Seriousness also comes through a sense of wonder. Familiarity, they tell me, breeds contempt. In some of our churches, we used to sing, "Tell me the old, old story" and the preachers would deliver as requested. In other churches, we listened patiently week by week to the same liturgy but if we're honest, we have to admit that, on occasion, we went through the motions with devotion and desire but left without ever experiencing any sense of wonder. Let me just show you why the Word of God is so wonderful. The prophets spoke of "the grace that was to come" (1 Pet. 1:10). Grace is God choosing to give us what we don't deserve for no other reason than He chose to do it. All that we are, all that we have, all that we ever hope to be, is because of the grace of God. In the fullest sense of the word, it is wonderful!

Christ's suffering should also lead to a sense of wonder. The inspired prophets were pointing to "the sufferings of Christ and the glory that would follow" (1:11). If we sit at Peter's feet for a few minutes, we will repeatedly hear the message of the wonders of God's grace and the immensity of Christ's suffering. I may lose my sense of wonder about the sufferings of Christ, but Peter never did. Perhaps he never forgot because his own behavior had intensified those sufferings. Christ's sufferings weren't just physical. Did you ever think of the horror of watching the sinless One being made sin, the eternal One suddenly being separated from the eternal Father and crying from the depths of His soul, "My God, my God, why have you forsaken me?" (Mark 15:34)? Did you ever try to imagine the sufferings of Christ when He watched His disciples as they forsook Him and fled, and Peter, the one who promised to be there, running away from the confrontation of a little girl?

It is easy to sing, "When I survey the wondrous cross on which the Prince of Glory died, my richest gain I count but loss and pour contempt on all my pride." But if I can survey the wondrous cross and lose the wonder, I've got a severe spiritual problem that is likely caused by some hardcore resistance; some deep seated sin that has calloused my heart.

Peter also talks about the wonder of the glories that would follow Christ's suffering and death. He was referring to the glorious resurrection, the glorious ascension and the glories of the coming Kingdom. All these subjects, he insists, were taught by the prophets. The contemporaries of Christ thought the Old Testament was teaching that the Kingdom would be on earth, that the blessing would be material and that the Messiah would be a great military conqueror who would get the Romans off their backs. They were excited about this possibility.

But Peter had learned that the truth was even more exciting. The Kingdom is not earthly, it's heavenly. The blessing is not material, it's spiritual. Our Lord wasn't getting the Romans off their backs. He was getting Satan off all our backs! And He is saying that if those people in the Old Testament had a sense of wonder, how much more should we? Prophets, angels and Old Testament saints with limited knowledge and experience, particularly compared to believers in the present age, were serious about God's salvation. So Peter's point is clear: we should be careful not to be casual about matters that others have regarded as crucial.

5

BEING HOLY!
1 PETER 1:13–16

It is very odd that the word *holy*—a word that has profound significance in the Bible—is not used very frequently even by Bible believers. They are familiar, of course, with the gold embossed HOLY BIBLE and will participate in HOLY COMMUNION and do, in some churches, celebrate HOLY WEEK. Otherwise the word is rarely used in everyday conversation. If that's the case in spiritual circles, it is not surprising then that the word is even less common in the average secular vocabulary. In fact if it does put in an appearance, it is often as a pejorative such as holy roller or a derogatory accusation that one is being holier than thou.

So bringing up the subject of holiness in either spiritual or secular communities can be difficult. However, when we consider that Scripture does say to followers of Jesus, "Be holy, says the Lord, because I am holy" (1:16), notwithstanding the difficulties, the confusion, the reticence on the part of many of God's people and the possible ridicule of others, we must try to deal with the subject of being holy.

Holiness Defined

The original meaning of the ancient biblical word translated as holy is "to be separated" or "to be cut off" and, accordingly, "to be different" and "to be distinct." God chose the word *holy* to describe Himself. He quite definitively states that "holy" is His name. When God attributes the name *holy* to Himself (and, incidentally, the expression "as he who called you is holy" in verse 15 can just as well mean, "Holy [that is His name] is the one who called you"), He is drawing attention to the fact that He is separate, different, distinct and transcendent. He is "totally other." This is the special meaning that begins to appear in Scripture concerning the word *holy*, and it relates first and foremost to God Himself. You'll remember, for instance, in Isaiah 6 that the prophet had a vision of heaven in which he saw the throne room, the Holy One sitting on the throne and the angelic beings singing, "Holy, holy, holy is the LORD Almighty" (Isa. 6:3). You may also recollect that when Joshua was speaking to his people and asking them to get their act together, they said that they would serve the Lord. Joshua was skeptical and replied, "You are not able to serve the LORD. He is a holy God" (see Josh. 24:15–19.) Apparently he thought they were being flippant in their response and lacking in the understanding of the otherness of God and the distinctly different lifestyle to which He was calling His people.

Further usage and development of the word began to include the idea "if God is holy, that which is identified with Him is also holy." The earliest illustration of this is in Genesis 2:3 where the Lord, having worked for six days and created all things, rested and declared the seventh day holy. Presumably, there were twenty-four hours like any other day and sixty minutes to every hour. The sun daily rose in the east and there was a normal sunset in the west. The only different thing about it was that now it was the Lord's day. It had been set apart specifically for Him and, accordingly, it was different or holy. (Incidentally, that's how we got our word holiday. Holidays used to be holy days in that they were set apart for worship and recreation.) As we develop this idea in Scripture, we see that not only days and things are set aside for the Holy One but also people are set apart and are called holy people. This, of course, is one of the powerful statements that Peter makes further on in his epistle—that Christians are holy people. That is, they have responded to the call to identify with the Holy One and therefore they are in God's eyes a different, separate and distinct people. They are "the people of God" (2:10).

This brings us to the ethical meaning of the word. The people of God have been declared by Him holy and are to be clearly distinguishable as they exhibit distinctive lifestyles based on ethical considerations derived from the Holy One. God—the Holy One—says what ought to be done because He is the one who decides what is right and wrong and He is the source of all morality and ethics. In short, once a believer acknowledges that he or she is a holy person because of his or her identification with the Holy One, and is required to live a holy life based on a holy ethic, he or she will begin to understand what it means to be holy.

This idea can be seen clearly in the Old Testament, but with a certain ceremonial emphasis. For example, in

Leviticus, God says to His people, "Be holy because I, the LORD your God, am holy" (19:2). And He promptly gives them instructions, some of which seem very odd to us in the present day. He forbade them to wear a garment made up of two kinds of material. That sounds absolutely ludicrous to us but think about it for a minute. If they had a garment made up of two kinds of material, it meant that they probably used the material that was available in their own land but mixed it with material from elsewhere. By doing so, they were mixing something that stood for the Lord with something that was opposed to the Lord. It seems a non-issue to us but in their ceremonial way of life, it was very important.

The clothes they wore were demonstrations of their identification with the Lord, His land and that which His land produced. If they could not manage on the Lord's provision, they didn't want anything to do with anything else. They were separate. They were distinct. They were other. They were a people set apart. They were a holy people. And so the ceremonial law developed from that.

When we get into the New Testament, we discover that the emphasis switched from outward ceremony to a change of the heart attitude. In the Old Testament, the difference was, to a large extent, seen by the outside; their externals. In the New Testament, there was a tremendous emphasis on an internal heart transformation. New Testament holiness of the heart (the work of the Holy spirit) produces holy people who will desire what the Holy One desires and act upon what the Holy One was requiring of them.

Holiness Desired

For many, there is no great desire to be holy. Too many people who want to be saved, to go to heaven, to be happy, to be healthy, to be wealthy and maybe even wise, don't see holiness as a priority! So let's ask ourselves, "What are the factors that motivate modern people towards holiness?" There are five that I can identify in this passage.

The first one is the character of God. God says on numerous occasions, and Peter quotes from the Old Testament, "Be holy, because I am holy" (1:16). We might be tempted to ask God, "God, why did you tell me to be holy?" His answer is likely to be very simple: "Because I am." The greatest motivational factor toward holiness for the believer ought to be the character of God. God revealed Himself to us, we liked what we saw and we made a decision. Nobody held a gun to our heads. Drawn by the gracious ministry of the Holy Spirit, we freely decided to be the Lord's. Those of us who freely choose to identify with the Lord must continually remember who the Lord is—the Holy One. We must be reasonable and recognize that there must be something attractive about His holiness. Otherwise, we wouldn't have been foolish enough to identify with Him. In other words, the character of God that drew us to Him is holiness and, therefore, if holiness is so attractive, how can we walk away from it in our own lives? The second thing that motivates us toward holiness is the call of God. You will notice that Peter says, "As he who called you is holy, so be holy in all you do" (1:15). God wants us to be united to Him. He calls us to relationship. He calls us to Himself. He calls us into a fellowship with His Son that ultimately leads us to finally being like Him! (see 1 Cor. 1:9; 1 John 3:2). This was His call; the call to which we responded. We must constantly remember that the call is based on His terms—not ours!

My youngest son, Pete, grew a beard in high school. He was going out for the basketball team, and he was favored to make the team. He worked through the summer and attended the practice sessions, and then the big day arrived when the cuts were coming. He survived them all! On the day a photographer came to take the varsity basketball team picture, Pete was told to sit on the side. When he asked the coach why he wasn't included in the picture he was told, "We don't want any hairy monsters in our picture." The coach added, "If you want to play on this team, you get rid of that beard. If you want the beard, you don't play on this team. It's as simple as that." Pete didn't have any problem with that. In fact, he retained a sense of humor and came home and said, "Dad, what must I do to be shaved?!"

I suppose Pete could have mirrored the present age and said, "If I want to grow a beard, I can grow a beard. I also feel I'm being discriminated against, so I'm going to get an attorney who will protect my constitutional rights I'm going to kick up a stink and I'll get this whole athletic program closed." But he didn't. He understood that if he wanted to be on the team, this was the way his coach was going to play the game, and Pete was going to play it his way. He shaved off his beard and played very happily for the team and coach.

The third factor in holiness is God's command. If God's character and call aren't enough for you, then how about His command? A good friend of mine recently said to me, "I get so confused about the whole subject of prayer I just say to myself, 'Why bother doing it?'"

So I answered, "It's easy to answer that one and I appreciate easy questions because I usually get hard ones."

He asked, "What's easy about that question?"

I said, "The easy answer to the question is, you pray because He told you to."

It's the same way with holiness. We may not understand holiness, we may not appreciate holiness, we may not even like holiness, but that's all delightfully irrelevant because He told us to be holy anyway! Granted, reluctant obedience is not what God is looking for but on occasion a joyful response to a challenging call is not always easily available. Even then though, we obey because He is Lord.

The fourth factor is the consistency of God. Holiness is not something that God has recently sprung on us. Throughout the Old Testament, God revealed Himself as holy, made holy demands upon His people, set them apart as holy and gave them the means to be holy. He showed them the advantages of holiness and the consequences if they refuse to be holy. He's had one basic, fundamental message right down through His dealings with humanity. The consistency of God is such that nobody can ever say, "I didn't know I was supposed to be holy. This is the small print on the bottom of the policy." We can't say that kind of thing if we've even begun to start thinking through who God is and what He has consistently been saying.

Finally, we need to be holy because it is the choice of God. Notice the word "therefore" (1:13). It links the passage we're talking about with the previous verses that describe the salvation that is available to us. The apostle reminds us that in the light of God's choice to provide His salvation, we must always remember that the salvation we enjoy includes holiness.

Lee Iacocca, former chairman of the board at Chrysler in the 1980s, told employees who were resisting a proposed wage freeze, "Good jobs at $17.50 per hour we have in plenty. Jobs at $20.00 per hour, we don't have. It's as simple as that." His position was very clear. At the risk of confusing God with Lee Iacocca, and the purposes of God with Chrysler Motor Corporation, workers at Chrysler and servants of God have this in common—their choices are limited by the choices of those in charge. The choice of God, His consistency, His command, His call and His character all point to the necessity for holiness. Reasons enough to encourage a serious exploration of this aspect of the believer's calling.

But there are major factors that hinder the pursuit of holiness. We may call three of them an unholy trinity—the world, the flesh and the devil. The devil rebelled against the Father and has not stopped rebelling against Him since that time. He is utterly and totally opposed to all the Father is and all the Father stands for. He is against the Holy One, therefore, you can be sure he is dead set against holiness.

Not only that, we recognize that the world crucified the Son. Somebody asked me the other day, "If Jesus came back today, would they crucify Him?" I said, "Probably not, it's not part of our culture as it was in Rome's day. But fallen man would find another way of getting rid of Him." The world and its system has always been fundamentally opposed to all that Christ represents. As we live our lives in this world, we must reckon with secular hostility to holy aspirations.

In addition, we have within us the flesh, which the Scriptures say fights against the Spirit (see Gal. 5:16–17). We have to recognize that we live our lives with the devil over us, the world around us and the flesh within us. When it comes to holiness we have much we're up against.

Holiness Developed

On the one hand, Scripture says that holiness is a position or status that is ours the moment we become Christ's. On the other hand, holiness is seen as a progressive development in our lives. When we talk about holiness being developed, we're talking about that ongoing growth of a life that is distinctive and different and separated unto God. There are two major ingredients to this: the divine and the human.

The divine ingredient of holiness is the ministry of the Holy Spirit. Peter called it "the sanctifying work of the Spirit" (1:2). This sanctifying work is quite literally a "making holy" work of the Holy Spirit. He alerts us, for instance, to who the Father is, thus introducing us to ideas of holiness. He also points out to us the unholiness of the Evil One, the world around us, and the flesh within us. This Instructor brings conviction and concern, aspirations and longings and, of course, He is also the dynamic power without which holy aspirations become unholy frustrations. Paul reminded the Thessalonians, "God did not call us to be impure, but to live a holy life. Therefore, he who rejects this instruction does not reject man but God, who gives you his Holy Spirit" (1 Thess. 4:7–8). This emphasis is even more powerful when we note that the original language Paul used says, "Who gives us his Spirit—the Holy One!" The Holy One promotes holiness and produces it.

The first human ingredient is a well-ordered mind. This is clear from Peter's instruction, "Therefore, prepare your minds for action" (1:13). Literally Peter wrote, "gird up the loins of your mind" which might sound strange to western ears! But to eastern men like Peter, it was a telling figure of speech. Long robes hindered vigorous actions such as the hauling in of a net full of fish or, if we imagine this in a more recent scenario, running to catch a bus. So the prospective runner, or hauler, would have to bend down, pick up the hem of the robe, pull it up between the legs and tuck the material into the belt. That's how you gird up loins! Apparently Peter thought our minds sometimes are untidy, cluttered, hindered and less than optimally active. They needed to be tightened up and prepared for healthy and meaningful action. The metaphor is apt and when applied requires some good, solid thinking about the Holy One, and some serious guarding of our minds against contrary influences.

Later in this passage, Peter talks about living in ignorance. The good thing is, that is not a problem for those whose minds have been enlightened by God. But we may have an untidy or underutilized mind concerning the Lord. When we recognize this, remedial action is called for.

The second human ingredient is a well-disciplined life. The King James version of the Bible uses the word *sober*, which, unfortunately, has limited connotations. For many, sober means "don't get drunk" or "to go around with a long face" or both. But the New International Version says to "be self-controlled." This is a better translation, particularly in light of the unholy trinity's activity being so ferociously opposed to holy living. God has outlined His limits for us. These limits are not designed to spoil our fun, but to enrich our lives. There are certain things that God is against because God is holy. There are certain things that He is for, for the same reason. To identify with Christ means we are against what He is against and for what He is for. Once this is understood, we begin to gladly accept and appreciate His limits and live self-controlled lives within them. This is how we begin to develop holiness. It comes from a well-ordered mind and a well-disciplined life.

A well-defined goal is the third human ingredient in holiness. Peter says, "set your hope fully on the grace to be given you when Jesus Christ is revealed" (1:13). The goal of the Christian is to live and move toward the day when the Lord Jesus Christ will come again and receive to Himself those who have committed themselves to Him. He will take us to be with Him, and usher us into the presence of His Father. And when we see Him, we will be like Him and will live for all eternity in the full flow of our redeemed humanity—glorified in the presence of the Father. That's quite a goal! Once we get our minds well ordered, our lives well disciplined and our goals well defined, we will find one theme running through the whole of our lives—holiness, holiness, holiness. At that point, it becomes rather obvious that our goal is to be more and more like Him because we're looking forward more and more to being with Him. Now if we say we love the Lord but we don't want to be like Him, then we're a living contradiction.

The fourth human ingredient is a well-established conversion. The apostle adds, "As obedient children do not conform to the evil desires you had when you lived in ignorance" (1:14). Peter, at this point, calls Christians "obedient children" but Paul, writing to the believers in Ephesus said, "You are children of disobedience" (see Eph. 2:2, kjv). This is a monumental change of status. Before converting to Christ, we wanted to be disobedient, but now we want to be obedient. That's one way we can tell if we're converted or not. We don't have to look for a dramatic experience so much as a change of attitude. And, in addition, a change of understanding. We used to live in ignorance, but now we have begun to understand. Then there is a change of desire. Before we just had evil desires to do our own thing, our own way. We desired to be our own person and indulge our own passions, but now, we're done with all that.

To be holy, then, is not to be stale and sterile, solemn and suspicious, but rather to be refreshingly, distinctly different. Not the bizarre difference of eccentricity or the contrived self-conscious difference of faddism, but the difference that comes from a heart in tune with a refreshingly different God.

6

A SENSE OF VALUES

1 Peter 1:17–25

The Circus Maximus in the Rome of Peter's day was big enough to contain half as many people as the Rose Bowl in Pasadena. Shortly after Peter's time, it was enlarged to hold a quarter of a million people. The streets, temples and palaces thronged with people from every corner of the globe. All roads, in those days, led to Rome. It was a remarkable city, the center of a vast empire, and yet, Peter appears to be decidedly underwhelmed about this empire and all its vast glories and achievements.

Nero, the emperor at that time, had awesome powers that, when married to his bizarre brutality, made him a fearsome opponent. Despite this, he apparently held no great terror for Peter. Peter knew what the Lord had told him about his own death, and he probably sensed that he didn't have long to go. Yet, he was not at all terrified by Nero. He was neither overwhelmed by the glory and majesty of the empire, nor threatened by the power and fury of the emperor. He didn't want the early Christians to be either. Peter's approach to life and death, power and glory, pain and suffering, success and failure was governed by a special set of values which he endeavored to teach the believers living in Roman provinces.

There are several important things we must notice concerning these values.

Certain Things Must Be Underlined

External appearances are deceptive. First Peter 1:17 states: "You call on a Father who judges each man's work impartially." The word translated *impartially* here is related to the Greek word for mask. In other words, God is not fooled by the masks we wear, or misled by the makeup we put on. He does not look on the outside but the inside.

When Samuel was sent to find a king for Israel, God warned him not to judge as man judges. Peter learned this lesson the hard way. One day he was having his quiet time on the roof and he fell asleep! God was not able to communicate with him through scripture or his study notes so He got through to him via a vision. In the vision Peter saw a great sheet, full of all kinds of animals, let down in front of his eyes. The Lord said to the apostle, "Get up, Peter. Kill and eat" (Acts 10:13).

Peter was horrified that the Lord apparently didn't understand about kosher laws and he said that he couldn't possibly eat unclean food to which the Lord replied, "Do not call anything impure that God has made clean" (10:15). I'm sure Peter didn't know why he received this vision until some Gentiles arrived at his front door and asked him to accompany them to the home of a Roman centurion named Cornelius. Up until that time, Peter had no dealings with

Gentiles. He would never enter a Gentile home because it would be unclean to him. But God was essentially saying to him in the vision, "Don't evaluate by externals, Peter. You've got to understand that I'm reading the heart of this man." When Peter arrived in Cornelius' home and preached, the Holy Spirit fell upon those assembled and Peter said, "I now realize how true it is that God does not show favoritism" (Acts 10:34). The fact that he used a similar expression in his epistle many years later, shows that he had learned that you can make some serious mistakes on the basis of external evaluations.

Financial resources are perishable. Peter calls "silver and gold" perishable things. He was talking particularly about silver and gold coins. Precious metals obviously fluctuate in real value, and inflation can play havoc with wealth. But more importantly, Peter says that silver and gold coins have negligible redemptive value and even less eternal value. Unfortunately, in our society, we don't have a very healthy sense of values because we tend to assume that the answer to all our problems is to throw money at them. Peter is pointing out that these values are severely limited and need to be treated as such.

Traditional norms are suspect. He goes on to talk about "the empty way of life handed down to you from your forefathers" (1:18). This is a very striking thing for Peter to say because as a convinced, conservative, orthodox Jew he was very proud of the traditions of his forefathers. No doubt they were well-meaning men. They had introduced customs or beliefs that were intended to assist in explaining or illustrating deeper values. But as the years went by, their descendants forgot that the customs were intended to be aids and they began to substitute the aid for the end, the ritual for the reality. If we become locked into our traditions to the extent that they assume paramount importance, we may be utterly misled by them.

The Lord Jesus taught Peter much in this regard. I'm reminded of one instance when Jesus was at the Feast of Tabernacles. The high priest carried a pitcher down the steep incline to the spring of Gihon, stooped down and filled the pitcher with water. Then he returned up to the Temple area with the holiday crowds following him. Standing in a prominent place, the priest poured out the water in a solemn ceremony related to the commemoration of the hard days of wilderness living that God had enabled His people to survive. This ritual had existed for centuries and no doubt had lost its significance for many of the spectators.

The Lord Jesus, watching the water ceremony, stood up at that crucial moment and shouted, "If a man is thirsty, let him come to me and drink. Whoever believes in me . . . streams of living water will flow from within him" (John 7:37–38). You see, Jesus was saying, "Your ritual and your traditions, which came from your forefathers, point to me. I am the source of living water, but you're so wrapped up with your cultural traditions that you've forgotten the truth. You have substituted the ritual for the reality and you are putting trust in tradition."

Temporal issues are transient. There are two very interesting phrases in verse 20. Speaking of the Lord Jesus, Peter says, "He was chosen before the creation of the world, but was revealed in these last times." When we put the expressions "before the creation of the world" and "these last times" together, we generate a tremendous sense of time in opposition to eternity. We do not know how or when the worlds were made, but by faith we believe they were created by the Word of God. He, of course, existed before the creation, living in a state of continuous existence. When He chose to make time, He created something entirely new. He determined that time would not go on indefinitely; there would be an end to time—what the Bible calls "the last times." When we understand this, we recognize eternity but we also realize that we are terribly transient creatures of time. Therefore, if we're going to have a right sense of values, we dare not operate purely on the basis of the temporal. We must always think in terms of eternal values. Life is part of creation and time is part of creation. Today is part of the last times and soon, our concept of time will be over and we will be ushered into eternity to face the God who, before creation, already existed in eternal existence.

Spiritual experiences are confusing. The apostle says in verse 23, "You have been born again, not of perishable seed, but of imperishable, through the living and enduring word of God." The Word of God, when sown in people's hearts, brings forth life eternal and is imperishable. But there is such a thing as perishable seed that is not the truth. When it is sown in people's hearts, it brings to bear untold confusion. This is important because we need to remember that all spiritual experiences are not necessarily valid. It is possible, for instance, for there to be a pseudo-conversion which is nothing more than a change of lifestyle. People may give up unwholesome activities and begin to be better people.

However, this should never be confused with the miracle of regeneration that comes because the Holy Spirit has germinated the seed of the Word of God sown in people's lives. At the present time, there is a considerable propagation of the truth of the gospel but there is also a disconcerting proliferation of misinformation.

Recently I was invited to appear on a TV show in Milwaukee. The producers didn't really want me because they said, "He's just a pastor who will talk about Christianity, and who needs that?" However, these same producers arranged for an astrologer to make a daily appearance on that show because they regarded his contribution as more valid and realistic! We must be careful to recognize the seed being sown and the fruit being grown.

Mortal men are finite. Quoting Isaiah, Peter says, "All men are like grass and all their glory is like the flowers of the field; the grass withers and the flowers fall, but the word of the Lord stands forever" (1:24–25). When we get into trouble, we promptly look to a human to deliver us. We pin our hopes on him or her, but if he or she doesn't deliver, we get rid of the person and get someone else on whom to pin a whole new set of hopes. There is no question that some people are more obviously powerful than others as some grasses are more impressive than others. Since Peter expected Nero to do something crazy at any moment, he had no option but to recognize that Nero had awesome power. He was significant, but he was, in Peter's estimation, only significant grass. Likewise, we must put mortal mankind in perspective. He comes out of nowhere, shoots up, grows into significance, but soon he is gone, and the world will go on without him. Therefore, a realistic system of values recognizes that mankind is finite and limited.

Cultural glories are also ephemeral. Not only are men like grass but "all their glory is like the flowers of the field" (1:24). Peter had seen the Circus Maximus. He had visited the Forum and seen where Nero was building his artificial lakes. He understood that the emperor had plans to build a golden palace. He had traveled the roads the Romans had built, seen their empire and benefited from their laws. But Peter insisted that even such glory would pass away. We know that other cultures have failed. Some of us have traveled around the world and we've seen the relics and remnants of previous majestic cultures.

Hindsight helps us to see that previous cultures had the seeds of their destruction sown into their foundation. But for some reason, we believe that ours is different. Ours will be the first one that will survive. It will never become corrupt, will never decay and will never become like the flowers that are glorious but inevitably fall off the tree. We often deny that we feel this way about our culture, but our identification with it is a clearer indication of our attitude than our protestations.

If we're going to get our values right, we must not forget these things.

Certain Things Need to Be Understood

I want you to notice what Peter says about the fatherhood of God, the saviorhood of Christ and the brotherhood of believers.

The Fatherhood of God

"God is the Father who judges impartially," according to verse 17. Our society is quite open to hear about God provided He is innocuous and primarily committed to our well-being. But if we begin to talk in terms of a Father who judges all men's work impartially, a certain degree of discomfort becomes evident. Yet the clear teaching of Scripture is that all we have done and all that we are will come under the scrutiny of the eternal Father who will function as our judge. But there is another side of the coin. We not only have a Father who is a Judge but we have a Judge who is our Father. That helps a lot. To know that our lives will be brought under the scrutiny of the One who has offered to adopt us into His family is to add a fundamental concept to our value system.

God is also the "Father who hears compassionately." Peter, when he wrote, "You call on the Father," uses the same word Paul used when he stood trial and said, "I appeal to Caesar." For Paul, the response was immediate—"To Caesar you will go" (Acts 25:11–12). Any Roman appealing to Caesar was guaranteed a hearing. And so it is with God. Any believer "calling" on the Father has His full attention. He is committed to hearing us compassionately. When the going gets tough, we should concentrate not on ephemeral values, mortal man, financial resources or external appearances, but on the fatherhood of God, because He will judge impartially and always be committed to hearing us compassionately. God is also the Father who redeems eternally. In First Peter 1:19, we are told what God has done through "the precious blood of Christ, a lamb without blemish or defect." The word *redeemer* is related to the verb that means to ransom and emphasizes the price of deliverance or salvation. There is a sense in which our salvation is free, but that does not mean it is without cost. In the same way that the first law of economics states, "There is no free lunch," the first law of redemption is that free salvation costs the Father everything. And the glorious truth of the gospel proclaims that He chose to pay it.

God is the Father who plans sovereignty. Peter wrote, "He [Christ] was chosen before the creation of the world" (1:20). Some people believe that God had a Plan A and a Plan B. Plan A was that the Garden of Eden would be great, He would make man and give him woman and they would live happily ever after. Everybody would enjoy everybody. Then unfortunately, Plan A came apart at the seams so God put Plan B into operation. He sent Jesus, had Him die on the cross and then took Him back to heaven. However popular this idea may be, it does not agree with Scripture.

Before the foundation of the world, God had already ordained that Jesus should be the Lamb without defect and blemish who would die and take away the sins of the world. We will struggle with this truth if we look at it solely from a human point of view. I have heard people say, "You mean to tell me that God knew what man would do, but made us anyway, and allowed us to go wrong, knowing He already had the answer? That's weird!" It is weird. It is one of the sublime mysteries of the sovereign God. But when the going gets tough, it is wonderful to realize that you can trust in a Father who had the end of all things planned before the beginning.

God is also the Father who triumphed gloriously. Verse 21 goes on to say, "Through him you believe in God, who raised him from the dead and glorified him." What else did God do? He raised Christ from the dead, took Him to His own right hand, gave Him great glory and told Him to wait until His enemies are made His footstool. So Jesus triumphed over sin, death, hell, the devil and all evil, and He is totally committed to doing exactly that—making all His enemies His footstool. Ultimately, God will be revealed on a cosmic, eternal scale as the One who is "All in all." The One who has triumphed gloriously. This is our sovereign, compassionate, eternal Father.

In changing times, when nothing seems certain any more, God will not change. So our "faith and hope are in [Him]" (1: 21).

The Saviorhood of Christ

We need to recognize the substitutionary aspect of what I call, the saviorhood of Christ. Peter, drawing from the rich heritage of the Old Testament, considers the Passover Lamb that was carefully nurtured and scrutinized, to make sure that it was without defect, before being offered for the sins of the people.

In this ancient ritual, he sees a picture of the Lord Jesus, who for thirty-three years was scrutinized and criticized and seen to be without defect. He was shown to be the spotless Son of God who voluntarily died as a substitute, like the lamb in the Old Testament. Innocent, blameless, without blemish, the lamb dies on behalf of the people that their sins might be forgiven. So Christ, blameless, died not for His sin but died as a substitute for the sins of the world. He died that we might be saved.

Then there is the saving aspect of the saviorhood of Christ. The word *redeemed* in these verses means "to release by paying a ransom." When the Iranians held fifty-two American hostages, they asked for a 24 billion dollars ransom. There was a long standoff and deadlock at this point, the result being that they didn't get the money and we didn't get the hostages. If the Lord Jesus Christ had not laid down His life as a ransom for billions of people, the standoff would have been understandable. But, in our case, the ransom was paid and the deliverance secured.

The Brotherhood of Believers

The apostle makes a strong statement in verses 22 and 23 concerning the behavior of the believers: "Now that you have purified yourselves by obeying the truth so that you have sincere love for your brothers, love one another deeply, from the heart. For you have been born again." The sheer value of the community of believers must never be overlooked. Sometimes the believer-to-believer relationship is similar to the relationship of pool balls to pool tables. We all have our identity—our own specific colors. We all sit on the same table. Often we're propelled around the fellowship and as we ricochet off the cushions, we bang into each other. But as soon as we touch, we use the momentum of our contact to head us off in opposite directions again. This will go on until someone slips off into the pocket and we give him a good funeral and say nice things about his life of colorful collision. Perhaps we need to better recognize how vital the brotherhood of believers is to our spiritual experience. I am sure Peter places this truth alongside the fatherhood of God and the saviorhood of Christ to highlight dramatically the significance of our relationships with other believers.

We all appeal to the same Father. We all have been born of the same seed (see 1:23). We have all "purified [ourselves] by obeying the truth" (1:22). In other words, we enjoy the same life, and we accept the same truth. We seek to obey because we know the same Father through the same Son. Because we have all these things in common, we share the same love, the same truth, and we experience the same redemption. It is in the community of this unity that there is strength. These are the values we build on if we are to live adequately in hard times.

Certain Tasks Must Be Undertaken

The first task in value building is the development of a reverent lifestyle. Again, verse 17 says, "Since you call on a Father who judges each man's work impartially, live your lives as strangers here in reverent fear." To develop a reverent lifestyle means to fear doing damage to the life of the brotherhood, the reputation of the Father, or the gospel of the Son. It also means that we should become decidedly irreverent about many things that other people revere. How often do we revere too many empty, useless traditions? How often do we treat with tremendous solemnity that which is really inconsequential? It seems that sometimes we're remarkably casual about the Father, the Son and the fellowship, and deeply in awe of things that have little intrinsic value and no lasting significance.

The second task is the development of a confident attitude. Peter, having outlined what the Father has done through the Son, reminds us that our faith and hope should be in God (see 1:21). Christians should be incorrigibly confident. However, self-confidence is not what Peter had in mind. He had been an expert in that field for a number of years and had proved many times the misplacement of that kind of confidence. Since coming to know the One he was writing about in his epistle, his own basis of confidence had been altered as thoroughly as the results of this change had been demonstrated dramatically. And he wished nothing less for all believers. The third task is developing a fervent relationship. Peter goes on, "Now that you have purified yourselves by obeying the truth so that you have sincere love for your brothers, love one another deeply, from the heart" (1:22). The building of relationships, like the construction of anything of value, takes time and effort. But the caliber of our relationships require a fervency of spirit that will be as demanding as the results of such fellowship will be rewarding. Only those who commit themselves to such a task will be able to access the resources of God available for troubled people in troubling times.

7

SPIRITUAL GROWTH

1 Peter 2:1–3

Toughness and tension are related. When I injured a leg running, the muscles deteriorated until it was necessary for me to go through a series of isometric exercises. The exercises, through tension, built up the muscles. In the same way, tense times make tough believers. It is also true that tense times require mature behavior from believers, and Peter, knowing this, addressed the subject of spiritual growth that leads to more mature behavior.

The Initiation of Spiritual Growth

There are four things that Peter mentions which are related to the initiation of spiritual growth. First, there is the proclamation of the Word of God. The previous chapter of the epistle concluded with "the word of the Lord stands forever. . . . And this is the word that was preached to you" (1:25). Peter had already stated the Word of God was like a seed that, when planted in the warm fertile soil of a receptive heart, brought forth life. Sometimes when we listen to the Word of God we behave as if we are evaluating it.

But that's like saying that soil evaluates the seed. When we put seed in soil, it's the seed that evaluates the soil. This is the thrust of the Parable of the Sower with which Peter was no doubt familiar (see Luke 8:5–15). People in the Roman provinces had proven to be receptive to the Word and had made a good start in their spiritual life and growth. This reminds us that there is no substitute in spiritual experience for the proclamation of and response to the seed of the Word of God.

Second, Peter notes the introduction to the Son of God. There is a simple instruction in Psalm 34:8 that says, "Taste and see that the LORD is good." Presumably Peter was thinking of this when he told his readers, "You have tasted that the Lord is good" (2:3). When the Word of God is presented it is like a meal being placed on the table. It is not enough to be told by way of proclamation, "This is good!" The real benefit comes from tasting. When we receive a presentation of the Lord Jesus, we are required to trust and obey Him. As we do this, we "taste of Him" and we come into the good of all that He has promised. We begin to discover the reality of His forgiveness, the sheer love that He has for us, and His power in our lives. In other words, we are introduced to the Lord and we taste and see that He is good.

Third, there is the reception of the life of God. In his first epistle, Peter says, "You have been born again" (1:23) and in the second epistle he says we "participate in the divine nature" (2 Pet. 1:4). Both expressions point to the fact that we experience the indwelling presence of the Lord Jesus who died and rose again for us. By the Proclamation of the Word of God, we are initiated into all that God has to teach us. In our introduction to the Son of God, we're initiated into a divine/human relationship. And through the reception of the life of God, we are introduced to the possibilities of a totally new life; a life lived in the power of His indwelling presence. Fourth, Peter notes the recognition of the people of God. In England, if somebody ever got a little arrogant and self-centered, we used to say to them, "Remember, you're not the only pebble on the beach." Sometimes in our spiritual experience we act as if we are the only person related to the Lord. But we must remember that God is bringing thousands, if not millions, of people to Himself. All these "born ones" have the same Father, acknowledge the same Son, are indwelt by the same Spirit, enjoy the same life and are related to each other. If we have come into an experience of the truth as it is in the Lord Jesus, we come into an experience of all the other people who are experiencing the truth too. That is why Peter calls us "brothers" and insists that "sincere love" characterize the relationship. Like infants placed in a family so they might be raised, the spiritual infant is placed among more mature believers, called the family of God, so that through relationship they may grow up into Christ.

The Stimulation of Spiritual Growth

There is a craving force that drives a hungry baby. Peter used the analogy brilliantly as he wrote, "Like newborn babies, crave pure spiritual milk, so that by it you may grow up in your salvation" (2:2). Believers ought to be stimulated to growth on an ongoing basis. The baby with no appetite is a sick baby. Likewise, those without appetites for spiritual growth are deficient in spiritual experience. A desire for growth needs to be stimulated.

You'll notice that the NIV bible says we are to "crave pure spiritual milk" (2:2). Some of you may be using the King James Version in which you'll find the familiar expression, "As newborn babies, desire the sincere milk of the word" (2:2). The Greek word for "word" is *logos*. Greeks, when they thought in terms of "word" (*logos*), also thought in terms of the reason behind the words. The reasonable, rational part of the human being was, in their thinking, the spiritual part. So when they used the word *logos* it could mean "word," "reason," "rationality" or "spirituality." All these things were wrapped up in the meaning. Hence the different translations from the Greek: "spiritual" in the NIV and "of the word" in the KJV. We will use this broader understanding of craving "spiritual milk" to point out four things that will stimulate valid spiritual growth. First, there is the stimulation by hearing the Word of God. If we understand that spiritual experience is initiated through the proclamation of the Word of God, we should find no difficulty understanding that spiritual growth is also related to the Word of God. There are three major ways in which an appetite can be stimulated through the Word of God. There is the attending to the preaching of the Word on a regular, thoughtful and prayerful basis. Second, we must have a personal daily devotional habit of feasting on the Word. Finally, we should participate with others in small groups or one-on-one situations where there can be a sharing of the Word. All these opportunities for growth ought to be warmly embraced. Second, stimulation happens by knowing the Son of God. Three ingredients are necessary if we are to know people. We need to talk to them. By talking, I mean having a dialogue. We listen to them so that we know what they are saying and feeling. We talk to them so that they know how we're responding to what they are saying. We also need to spend some time with them. This time needs to be what we, somewhat euphemistically, call "quality time." Quality time, from my experience, requires accessibility and availability—they have to be able to get to us. We finally need to trust people. It is only by trusting that we find out what people are made of. Dependability is demonstrated only by giving people the chance to let you down. Getting to know somebody better takes talk, time and trust.

Growth in the knowledge of Jesus is very similar. We must build into our lives the opportunity to talk with Him. Life situations where we have to trust Him must be welcomed rather than dreaded and avoided. Take time to be with Him in the quiet place but also learn to practice His presence in the busy places. When we are tempted to say there are not enough hours in a day, we must remember God has given the exact right number of hours to do what is necessary.

Third, stimulation is created by experiencing the life of God. It is all too easy to lower the sights of our Christian attainment so that we feel satisfied with our spiritual achievements. If we aim low enough, there is not the same fear of failure. This can lead to misplaced contentment and disinterest in spiritual growth. Let me give you an example. The Bible does not say "Rejoice in the Lord sometimes." What it actually says is, "Rejoice in the Lord always" (Phil. 4:4). The "always" requires a high aim. The "sometimes" is much more manageable. When I wake up on a nice morning I feel good, so I rejoice and I attribute it to the Lord. I say, "Good morning, Lord." I rejoice in Him. But when I wake up to eighteen inches of snow, fifteen degrees below zero, my car won't start, my boss chews me out and I can't watch Monday night football because I've got a meeting, rejoicing is not an option if I operate on a "sometimes" basis.

Suppose I decide to think, "The Bible says what it means and means what it says; therefore, it means rejoice in the Lord always and that's going to take more than I've got!" As soon as I come to that conclusion, I start being interested in more than my ability. The indwelling presence of the living Lord Jesus becomes a vital concern. If we lower our sights to the level of our attainment, all it takes to live it is ourselves. But if we raise our sights according to Scripture, all it takes to live it is ourselves related to Him. We create a desire for spiritual growth in terms of the life of God when we desire to live in accordance with God's Word, not according to carefully selected and revised portions.

Fourth, stimulation is created by relating to the people of God. It is possible to live our lives spiritually, alone. We do our own thing, we go our own way, we don't interfere with anybody and we don't let anybody interfere with us. But this doesn't promote much growth. The family is the place for growth. It's there that we really know who people are because they speak freely, react instinctively, relate honestly and live supportively. It is in that kind of an environment that we come to terms with ourselves, examine our exposed frailties and take steps to live harmoniously even with those with whom we find tension. The spiritual family is not just people in the pews on Sunday, sitting in a large crowd and retaining their anonymity. The true spiritual family is a group of believers that share mutual commitments and healthy interactions. In such an environment, it is easy to identify prejudices and presuppositions, weaknesses and strengths, gifts and the lack of them. We level with each other and confront each other, we correct each other and reprove, rebuke and encourage each other—and therein lies our growth.

The Consolidation of Spiritual Growth

Is it possible to measure spiritual growth? Can we know if we are growing up spiritually? Peter seemed to think so and he particularly addressed the subject of relationships. He said in verse 1, "Therefore, rid yourselves of all malice and all deceit, hypocrisy, envy, and slander of every kind." There is a definite link between tasting that the Lord is good, hearing the Word, being born again of the Spirit, craving spiritual milk and growing. In this context, Peter shows that growth is clearly measurable in relationships. This requires particular attention to identifying things that are wrong and dealing with them. We must recognize our own behavior. I have learned in my interpersonal relationships that very few other people perceive me to be what I perceive myself to be. In the same way, my perceptions of others are often far removed from their self-perceptions. We can recognize our behavior through the Word of God. Peter learned this the hard way. One day when Jesus told His disciples about His impending death and resurrection in Jerusalem, Peter interposed his considerable bulk between the Lord Jesus and the Holy City and said, "Not so, Lord." The response of the Lord Jesus practically blew Peter out of the water. Jesus said, "Out of my sight, Satan" (Matt. 16:23). Peter was doing what he thought was right. Possibly everybody else was thinking the same thing. But Peter didn't just think it, he spoke out! But he could not perceive what was behind his own behavior until Jesus, almost brutally, showed him the reality of his action. If we would carefully and assiduously put our behavior under the spotlight of the Word of God, we would have similar shocks to the one Peter experienced. We can also recognize our behavior through the example of the Lord Jesus. Peter went fishing with the Lord Jesus on one occasion. He was a good fisherman who knew exactly what he was doing, but that day, he caught nothing. Jesus suggested a different approach, an approach that Peter agreed to, and to his amazement the net came out so full of fish it began to break. Peter fell down in front of the Lord Jesus and said, "Go away from me, Lord; I am a sinful man" (Luke 5:8). This remarkable reaction was not triggered by a net full of fish but by the realization of who Jesus really was. A good way to evaluate our behavior, after we put it under the searchlight of the Word of God, is to put it alongside the example of Jesus Christ

We can recognize our behavior by our confrontations with believers. Peter was no stranger to confrontation. He was involved in the controversy about Gentile believers' responsibility to the Jewish religion. Unfortunately, he had said one thing and then done another, so his inconsistency compounded the problem. When Paul arrived on the scene, he read the situation and promptly set up a meeting with Peter. Paul "opposed him to his face" (Gal. 2:11). Confrontation among believers can be destructive or creative. Done in the wrong spirit, it can decimate a brother, but when done properly, it can bring forth positive results. I learned in the early days of my ministry that to confront people effectively and positively we must first earn the right to do so—by proving our love for those people.

We must also be willing to repent for our behavior. Psychologists and psychiatrists have greatly helped us to understand modern mankind. We know a lot more about human behavior than ever before, but unfortunately, some of the understandings are misunderstandings. A specialist in human behavior can identify the factors that lead to an action, but if he then assumes that the factors alone are to blame and the person is not responsible, he will arrive at a dangerous conclusion. He will see all actions as the result of circumstances rather than choice and, accordingly, prescribe therapy rather than repentance. That said, in many instances when spiritual therapy does include repentance for sin, repentant sinners could benefit greatly from therapy by dealing with the factors that led to the sin.

At some point, we must reject our ungodly behaviors. First, there is to be the rejection of malice. The Bible uses different Greek words to describe anger. There is the "short fuse" anger that is volcanic in nature and expressive. Then there is the "slow burn" anger that is a cold, hard, settled resentment devoted to getting even. The latter is malice, and it must be rejected—thrown away like dirty clothes. How is it done? By a commitment to help the one who harmed us rather than adding more harm to the harm done.

Second, we must reject guile. Guile is a desire to deceive or to mislead. Sometimes we do it because honesty is too painful. Rather than telling the truth in love, something that might help to heal the situation, we often take a line that is perilously close to "lying lovingly!" Guile is often just lying dressed in Sunday clothes, but those too need to be ripped off!

Third, we should reject hypocrisy. Hypocrisy is playact-ing. It is being one thing inside and another thing outside. Why do we do it? Because we want people to think highly of us and we fear the truth may be so unpleasant that we will lose their love and respect. But this attitude is not con-ducive to growth. It must be rejected. Instead of having an inordinate tendency to conceal, we must recognize the ne-cessity to confess when it is called for and appropriate.

Fourth, let's reject envy. Envy is resentment that anoth-er person is or has something you neither are nor have. Peter was possibly threatened by John because he was young and smart and special to Christ. When he was told how he would die, he immediately asked, pointing to John, "What about him?" The Lord gave him some very helpful advice, telling him in effect, "Peter, you have only got two things to do. Number one, mind your own business and number two, follow Me" (see John 21:21–22). That's the best advice on how to handle envy!

Fifth, reject slander. Slander is speaking against some-body. It is dangerous, destructive and despicable. It must be discarded. Some simple rules help in this difficult assignment. Before speaking against somebody, ask yourself, "Is it true—really true? How do I know it's true?" Next, "Is it fair? Is it only partially true—selectively indifferent to some pieces of data?" Finally, "Is it necessary? What will the sharing of this information achieve that is constructive?" One of the best ways of helping other people to reject slander is to stop listening to them!

Spiritual growth is the evidence of life and health in the Spirit. Having been initiated, it must be stimulated in order to be consolidated. Interpersonal relationships are often the best indicators of spiritual growth or the lack thereof.

8

BUILDING ON THE ROCK
1 Peter 2:4–8

Long before he was Peter, the Galilean fisherman was called Simeon (also known as the Greek equivalent, Simon). In addition, his Aramaic name was Cephas. The Lord Jesus added to his impressive array of names by also calling him Petros (the masculine equivalent of the feminine Greek word "Petra"). Petros means a rock! And of course, Peter is the English and German equivalent of Petros.

The Lord made a very powerful statement concerning Peter being the rock when He said, "You are Peter, and on this rock I will build my church" (Matt. 16:18). This statement has given theologians grounds for debate ever since. Roman Catholic theologians insist that the Lord Jesus was saying that Peter was the rock on which the church was going to be built and on this premise have added numerous traditions concerning church governance and other important issues. Some Protestants object to this interpretation and its resultant traditions and insist "the rock" was not Peter but the confession that Peter made that Jesus was the Christ. We don't need to get into this discussion because Peter was clearly a leader in the group of apostles and they were called the foundation of the church (see Eph. 2:20). In addition we do know that Peter called Jesus "the living Stone," the "cornerstone" and the "capstone" (2:4, 6–7). He also added that all believers are "like living stones" (2:5) built upon the living Stone in order that we might become an edifice in which God dwells by His Spirit. There is therefore no question that human agencies like Peter and the Apostles were involved in building the church but it is Christ Himself who is the Rock, the living Stone. When the going gets tough, it's very important that we have a solid foundation under our feet. The Lord told us about the man who built a beautiful house on sand but when the wind came the house fell down (see Matt. 7:24–27). Then, in contrast, He talked about the man who built his house on the rock—the same kind of house, wind and waves—but this house stood firm. When the going gets tough, many people collapse because they have built a magnificent edifice on sand. It is important that we check how we're building, what we're building and where we're building. Peter tells us that we need to build on the Rock, and that Rock is Christ.

Christ The Living Stone

When we talk about Christ, the living Stone, we are thinking of Christ in a particular capacity. In order to understand this, there are three things we need to examine. First, in the Old Testament there is a prophetic pronouncement concerning the living Stone. The prophet Isaiah wrote: "The LORD Almighty is the one you are to regard as holy, he is the one you are to fear, he is the one you are to dread, and he will be a sanctuary; but for both houses of Israel he will be a stone that causes men to stumble and a rock that makes them fall" (Isa. 8:13–14). He was telling them what they ought to fear and what they ought not to fear. He told those who were worried about a political conspiracy, the economic conditions and societal problems not to worry about such things, but rather to fear the Lord, because their problems were fundamentally spiritual rather than political or societal. Those who fear the Lord will find Him to be a sanctuary, but those who disregard Him in their obsession with more mundane matters will stumble and fall when they face His judgment. He, to them, will be a stumbling stone.

The prophet later returned to his theme saying: "See, I lay a stone in Zion, a tested stone, a precious cornerstone for a sure foundation; the one who trusts will never be dismayed" (28:16). Isaiah's contemporaries were all confused, taking refuge in untruth, and living in a fantasy world. They disregarded absolute standards and lived in a maze of relativity. But in the midst of the confusion, God had put a Rock that was absolutely true and stable—the standard of righteousness and the basis of justice.

When we turn to Psalm 118, which was sung by the pilgrims climbing the steep ascent to the Temple in Jerusalem, we read: "The stone the builders rejected has become the capstone; the LORD has done this, and it is marvelous in our eyes. This is the day the LORD has made; let us rejoice and be glad in it" (Ps. 118:22–24). We are not certain when this psalm of jubilation was written so we cannot identify the rejected stone that became the cornerstone with any certainty. Some use this as a reference to the fact that the Temple, which was David's idea, was built even though God rejected David's request to build it. Others see it as a reference to the Temple being rebuilt after it was destroyed when the people of God were humiliated by their enemies. Either way, the theme is the same: jubilation because God restored what He had judged. The rock in the Old Testament is therefore a symbol of judgment, justice and jubilation.

Second, when we turn to the New Testament, we find in Mark 12 a messianic parable. The Lord told a story of a man who planted a vineyard, put a wall around it, dug a pit for the winepress, built a watchtower, rented the vineyard to some farmers and went away on a journey. At harvest time, he sent a servant to collect the rent (a portion of the fruit) but the farmers seized him, beat him up and sent him away empty handed.

The owner sent further emissaries who were also treated with increasing violence and rejection. Finally, the owner sent his son, believing his tenants would respect him. But they killed him too! Having told this parable, the Lord linked it with the stone the builders rejected which became the capstone, and then showed that He was both the Old Testament Stone and the New Testament Son. He was laying claim to being the basis of judgment and justice and jubilation. He was the One of whom the prophets spoke, none other than the Son rejected by the tenants but accepted by the Father and promised to be the chief cornerstone (see Mark 12:1–11).

Third, we need to look for the apostolic teaching. In Acts 4 we find Peter preaching before the Sanhedrin. He is in trouble because he healed someone, and the authorities are asking, "By what power or what name did you [heal this man]?" His answer was straightforward: "By the name of Jesus Christ of Nazareth, whom you crucified but whom God raised from the dead . . . this man stands before you healed. He is 'the stone you builders rejected, which has become the capstone'" (Acts 4:7–11). If we weren't sure of the prophetic pronouncement and if we had a problem with the messianic parable, we shouldn't have any difficulty with the apostolic teaching! The rejected stone, Peter says, is the crucified Christ. The capstone is Christ exalted.

Let me explain more about the capstone. The builders of Solomon's Temple were given the instruction that no sound of tools was to be heard at the Temple site. So all the stones were cut out of the quarry, dressed, shaped, transported and immediately put into place. These immense stones had to be cut exactly right, and without plaster or cement, they had to fit together.

The secret was the capstone! The capstone was the final unit that was intricately cut, beveled and angled. It was uniquely fitted for its crucial role of holding the whole edifice together. Like a jigsaw puzzle holds together when the last piece fits, so the capstone brought everything together. And only the stone especially prepared would fit. This stone, Peter told the Sanhedrin, is Jesus—rejected, crucified, risen and exalted.

Christ is also the cornerstone. He is the foundation of the main corner upon which everything is built. Jesus Christ is the One upon whom God has built everything. Peter puts it this way: "Salvation is found in no one else, for there is no other name under heaven given to men by which we must be saved" (Acts 4:12). In our contemporary world, there are attempts to take the best of Christianity, Buddhism, Islam, Hinduism, Shintoism and other religions, bring them together and make out of them a universal religion where everybody can be together and everybody can believe the same thing. The problem for Christians is that the apostles taught that Christ and Christ alone is the rock upon which God is building everything, that Christ and Christ alone is the capstone that will make everything fit together, and there is salvation in no other.

When we approach Christ as the living Stone we need to draw from Peter's rich knowledge of the Old Testament. The children of Israel, traveling through the wilderness, were thirsty and disgruntled. God told Moses to go to a rock, smite it with his rod and out of the rock waters would flow. It became a living stone; a living rock. There was a tradition among the Hebrews that this rock followed them in the wilderness, and you'll find Paul using this idea in First Corinthians 10, where he says this living rock is Christ. In this way, we see another picture of Christ as the living Stone from whom life originates. Spiritual life and nourishment are to be found in Him and Him alone. As we stated in a previous chapter, during the Feast of Tabernacles the people went to Jerusalem to commemorate the time when their forefathers were in the wilderness and Moses smote the rock from which the water flowed. The chief priest standing before the assembled congregation poured water that had been collected from the spring out of a pitcher. Likewise, on another occasion,

Christ shouted from the crowd, "If a man is thirsty, let him come to me and drink. Whoever believes in me . . . streams of living water will flow from within him" (John 7:37–38). He was insisting that He was the reality behind the ritual; the substance behind the symbol. He was the Rock from whom the living waters come.

Peter points out, however, that this stone can also be a stumbling stone to some people. Those who reject Christ, who aren't going to move or change, will stumble over Him and fall into that spiritual lost-ness, I mentioned before. This, in essence, is the divine revelation of the living stone, the corner stone, the living rock. It is the prophetic, messianic and the apostolic revelation.

Now let's look at the human reaction to all this. We talk a lot about human freedom and human rights, and we must remember that we have them because they were God-ordained. One of the greatest rights we have is the freedom to react to what God has revealed. Peter says that some people "stumble because they disobey the message—which is also what they were destined for" (1 Pet. 2:8). It's interesting to notice that the Greek word that is translated as *destined* is the same one that is translated as *lay*. In the same way that the builder lays the foundation stone and it is settled in the place of his choice, so God has "settled" the consequences of mankind's choices. We are free to react as we wish to the message of Christ, the living Stone. But God has the absolute right to determine the consequences of our choices. God has reserved for mankind the freedom to choose and has reserved for Himself the freedom to determine the consequences of that choice. He has laid it like a rock—there it stands! Nothing will change it. God has ordained that those who respond to the message of the Living Stone will find that, as they build their lives on Him, they will never be put to shame. There is utter security in Him. On the other hand, God says that those who choose to reject Him will find a stone of stumbling instead of a stone of security. They'll stub their toes on Him every day. They'll bump up against His truth constantly. They'll trip over the convicting work of the Holy Spirit and stumble over the barriers that God is putting in their pathway to hell. But they'll go on tripping, stumbling and falling until in the end they will fall, still rejecting Him, into a lost eternity.

Christians: The Living Stones

Having developed one application of the living Stone, Peter goes on to develop another. He writes, "You also, like living stones, are being built into a spiritual house to be a holy priesthood, offering spiritual sacrifices acceptable to God through Jesus Christ" (2:5). This means, first of all, that the Lord Jesus wants to have a very special relationship with those who choose to be related to Him. In the same way that He is called the living Stone, He calls us to be "like living stones" too. This reminds me of what He said about being the light of the world. He said, "So long as I am in the world, I am the light of the world." But then he added to His disciples, "You are the light of the world" (See John 8:12; 9:15; Matt. 5:14). In short, when we become believers, we are called to perpetuate that which Christ started, to project that which Christ is. He is the Light but we become the lights of the world. He is the living Stone but after He is gone, we become the living stones. So we establish a very definite and simple relationship with Him. The abc's of this relationship is as follows:

A. We admit: We admit the truth concerning Him and ourselves. Truth that we may have chosen to avoid. Truths that we may have resisted. We admit the truth of our spiritual condition and His saving merit.

B. We believe: We trust that what God says about ourselves is right. We trust that what God says about His Son is true. We come to believe deeply these things to such an extent that we stake everything on Him.

C. We come to Him: The only way that we can come is repentantly and submissively. We come to Him and say, "Lord Jesus, I am the sinner you died to save. I'm the rebel over whom you wish to reign. I am living out here in a cold, chaotic stone yard and I need to be built into who you are and to what you're doing. I come to you and I surrender myself to you."

D. We discover: We discover the reality of all the things Peter had been speaking and we join with him in proclaiming "This stone is precious" (2:7). Only those who believe find Christ infinitely precious. Only those who come to Him find Him infinitely rich. Only those to whom the Spirit of God is speaking find this truth overwhelmingly beautiful. We can always know if we've become a living stone built upon the living Stone by determining if Jesus Christ is precious to us. Living stones start to live like the living Stone. He is not only Savior and Lord but He is our model too. We aspire to be like Him.

Moreover, the apostle points out that living stones "are being built into a spiritual house" (2:5). This is a picture of the stones being cut in the quarry and built into a temple. The New Testament tells us quite clearly that individual believers are cut out of the quarry of society and transported into a place where their lives are fit together with other lives, and they are built into the church of Jesus Christ to be the temple of the Holy Spirit. God is alive in our midst and doing something to His glory and man's blessing. Peter was never one to worry about mixed metaphors! He said that we're not only the temple but we're the priests serving in the temple. We have become a holy priesthood. That means that every believer has a gift with which to develop a ministry.

Not only that, we engage in a life of spiritual sacrifice. A life of ministry is a life of sacrifice and service. Lives built on sand, crumble. Lives built on the Rock, triumph. Jesus Christ is either utter security or the basis of stumbling. Identified with Him, we become living stones, built up in a fellowship of believers, exercising a spiritual priesthood, engaging in a ministry and living a life of sacrifice. In turbulent times, we don't need sandstone; we need Christ—the Rock. And we need never wonder if we are built on Him because the evidence will be clear. When we are sure of our foundation, we have little to fear and tough times are nowhere near as tough.

9

GOD'S SUPPORT GROUP
1 Peter 2:9–12

There are few things worse than loneliness, especially when it manifests as us facing hard times alone. God never intended this for His creatures. He created us for relationships. And He certainly did not intend His redeemed children should find themselves alone in an extremity. His design for His children is that they should face hard times in the special community of the redeemed. Peter is careful to emphasize "the people" aspect of spiritual experience in his epistle.

He uses three different Greek words in these verses as he talks about a people, a race and a nation. His objective is to remind the believers of the strength and security to be found in shared experience and to highlight the rare privilege of belonging to God's people and sharing in their blessings. He uses a rich variety of words to describe this privilege. He says we are "a chosen people, a royal priesthood, a holy nation, a people belonging to God" (2: 9).

The Place of Privilege

Once more we find Peter drawing his ideas from the Old Testament. The expressions "chosen people, royal priesthood, holy nation and people belonging to God" are not original to Peter. They came from his study of Exodus 19 and Isaiah 43. But he does not hesitate to apply the ancient concepts of the people of God to Christian believers scattered throughout the Roman provinces. And of course, we should recognize that we follow in that sequence. There are two things we should notice about this place of privilege: the privilege of becoming a people and the privilege of being a priesthood.

There are a number of words used to describe the privilege of becoming a people. First of all, Peter calls us "a chosen people!" He has already told the people that they have been chosen according to the foreknowledge of God. God has always freely chosen to call "a people" to Himself. He chose to make from Abraham, a great people. He narrowed it down to Isaac, not Ishmael, and further determined to work through Jacob rather than Esau. The progeny of Jacob, whose name was changed to Israel, became known as the people of Israel. You might remember that He set His hand upon them, brought them out of Egypt and placed them in the land of promise. Then He said that they would function as a nation, as a people and as a race distinct from other nations. His objective was to clearly demonstrate to other nations what a nation is like when God is its Lord. They were a chosen people. There is a sense in which God chooses individuals to do certain things, but we need to bear in mind that God has actually chosen to work through "peoples" and communities. Individuals must see themselves as part of these bodies. The Preamble to the Constitution of the United States says, "We the people of the United States, in order to form a more perfect Union, establish Justice, ensure domestic Tranquility, provide for the common defense, promote the general Welfare, and secure the Blessings of Liberty to ourselves and our Posterity, do ordain and establish this Constitution of the United States of America." Notice that it is not a group of individuals saying, "Okay, gang, we're going to do our own thing. Let it all hang out. If it feels good, it must be right. Have fun!" This kind of thinking is a more recent development. If the United States had started off on that basis, frankly there would be no nation. There would not be "a people." Because there was a decision by a number of individuals to submerge their individuality for the common good, a nation was born.

God doesn't just call individuals to Himself to save them and let them do their own thing. Allow me to apply the precepts of the Constitution of the United States to the people of God without in any way confusing them. We could perhaps say that God calls individuals to be part of a people whose objective is to produce a more perfect union, to work toward the establishing of justice and righteousness and interpersonal relationships. When they sense that people in the fellowship are not enjoying domestic tranquility they commit themselves to assist in attaining it. If they recognize that some people are under attack, they commit themselves to the common defense. And if some are impoverished and some are in need and others have an abundance, they commit themselves to the general welfare of the fellowship of believers. This is the state of high privilege God has chosen for us. The community of the called is certainly not an exclusive club. It is a group of people committed to Christ and His people. God has chosen it to be this way.

Secondly, we are called "a holy people." We are already familiar with the word *holy* but we may remind ourselves that, in this context, it means that the people of God are a separate people. They have a distinctive identity. They see themselves as people called by God for special service. They regard themselves as the people of God with responsibilities and privileges quite different from the priorities of the world around them. Frequently they find themselves "out of step" with the surrounding culture. They behave in ways that are clearly different from many of the prevailing and accepted behavior patterns of the day. But the word *holy* also has the connotation of purity. Some of the things common to our world just don't belong in the people of God. When we identify with the people of God, there is a distinctive rejection of much that unbelievers condone and embrace. To engage in such things brings discredit to the people with whom we identify and harm to the name of the One to whom we owe allegiance.

Thirdly, we are called "a special people." Peter says we are "a people belonging to God" (2:9). This translation doesn't do justice to the word Peter used. When I was a small boy I learned a hymn that contained the words, "When He cometh, when He cometh to make up His jewels." I learned it so well, I can't remember it any more! I remember thinking about that hymn and saying to my mother, "Mother, who are Jesus' jewels?" And she said, "You are." So I strutted around like a little jewel for a while. Then I forgot all about it. Years later I was reading Malachi 3:17, "They will be mine . . . when I make up my jewels," and I realized that the hymn writer got his idea from Malachi. But so did Peter, for the word he uses is exactly the same as was used in the Greek translation of Malachi 3:17. The expression that says we are a people belonging to God means, literally, that we are purchased at tremendous cost and therefore are as precious as a jewel to His heart. We are a special people to God. We are precious!

Fourthly, we are "a called people." We are intended to "declare the praises of him who called [us] out of darkness into his wonderful light" (2:9). The "call" in this passage means to give a name. We often use the word *call* in this way. I am called Stuart Briscoe because I was born to Mary Elizabeth Briscoe and she and her husband, my father, chose to give me the first name Stuart. But the word *call* also means to invite somebody into an experience, a status or a position. So the call of God to individuals is that they might be invited from the position in which they find themselves in to a new situation where they will have a new name—His name. It is rather like being called out of darkness into His most marvelous light. The initiative or the call starts with God. It is He who calls, invites and invades our darkness. Charles Wesley said it wonderfully:

> "Long my imprisoned spirit lay,
> Fast bound in sin and nature's night,
> Thine eye diffused a quickening ray,

I woke, the dungeon flamed with light,
My chains fell off, My heart was free,
I rose, went forth and followed thee."

But God doesn't do it just for individuals. He does it for a people called together into this light.

Fifthly, we are "a pitied people" too. Peter writes: "Once you were not a people, but now you are the people of God; once you had not received mercy, but now you have received mercy" (2:10). This time he quotes Hosea 2:23 ("mercy" carries the connotation of "pity").

As Jesus and His disciples were coming out of Jericho, they met a blind man called Bartimaeus. When he realized Jesus was in the neighborhood he called out at the top of his voice, "Jesus, Son of David, have mercy on me!" (see Mark 10:46–52). In the modern world, not only is great emphasis placed on human rights but the extensive social services in place to meet the needs of those whose rights are not being met. It is therefore understandable that where there is a need, the meeting of that need is seen as a right that solidifies into an entitlement. But there is a danger that those who benefit from such largesse may possibly begin to see rights where they do not exist and become upset when imagined entitlements are not forthcoming. So it is in our dealings with God. There is a danger that we may imagine that we have an inalienable right to have God do for us things He has never promised us, which, in fact, He would never countenance! Bartimaeus having presumably heard that Jesus healed people might have assumed that he had the right to see and therefore healing was an entitlement!

But when he called out to Jesus, he made no such assumption. He didn't demand his rights, he pleaded for mercy! He asked the Lord to pity him in his invidious condition. To ask for mercy is to speak from a position of weakness. To elicit pity is to project a deep sense of unmet need. This is the only posture with which we can approach God.

Peter clearly understood this when he wrote, "Once you were not a people, but now you are the people of God; once you had not received mercy, but now you have received mercy" (2:10). The lovely thing about the people of God is that they have no pretensions because they know their only claim to fame is that they asked for mercy, God pitied them in their spiritual poverty and graciously met their needs.

Peter also talks about the privilege of being a "priesthood." The expression "royal priesthood" suggests that believers come together as a community around a king and, as a priesthood, engage in spiritual service.

Some segments of the church differentiate between the clergy and the laity. (Incidentally, one of the Greek words that is translated "people" in this passage is the word from which we get the word *laity*.) The clergy are respected as having received and responded to the call of God to specific service. They function as intermediaries who act on God's behalf for the people and on the people's behalf in their approach to God. There was a great emphasis on this for centuries. Sadly, sometimes church architecture keeps the clergy separate from the laity so that they have to peer over heads and hats and through ornate screens, into the dim distance, to where the clergy are doing religion for the people. But about five hundred years ago, as part of the

Reformation, there was a rediscovery of the Bible doctrine of the "priesthood of all believers." This did not mean that men and women called to serve the Lord in "professional" ministry no longer have a special place in the church. It meant that the church is a fellowship comprised of believers who are priests, all of whom have a ministry, exercise gifts and offer spiritual sacrifices to Him. We all are involved in building up the body of Christ.

We also are a kingdom, which means that we are called together, as Paul wrote, "[to] reign in life through the one man, Jesus Christ" (Rom. 5:17). This expression, a kingdom, suggests a realm of experience where the rule and reign of a king is recognized and respected. In the case of the church, a group of people who are called to stride through life with a regal bearing—not stumbling, not staggering, but striding over what other people sink under. We can't do it individually, but as a community of royalty and priests, we are a privileged people and uniquely equipped to live well in less than ideal circumstances. Peter, when he called believers "aliens and strangers in the world" (2:11), was reminding us that we must accept our status. He already mentioned this idea in the first chapter.

When we arrived from England almost fifty years ago, we were issued visas that stated we were "resident aliens" in the United States of America. It was very obvious that there was a difference between being a citizen and an alien. The former enjoys privileges and responsibilities the latter lacks. It's a matter of status; an issue of belonging. The alien is not "at home." The environment is different from all that he is used to. Life means something different in the new land as opposed to the old. Peter used the idea of believers as "aliens and strangers in the world" to stress the fact that if you are a member of the people of God, you are, to a certain extent, an alien and a stranger to the rest of society (which is what he meant by "world"). Part of the price believers pay for the privilege of being "a people" is that we are aliens among the citizens of this world. The status may be hard to live with at times. I was told on a number of occasions, when I raised a question about America, "If you don't like it here, why don't you go back to where you belong?!" But if we rejoice in being the people of God, we must accept the fact that our "other-worldly" status may generate suspicion, distrust or even outright antagonism. Being an alien is part of the territory.

When I was eighteen, I played on a rugby team for the Royal Marines. The rugby was great, but the time after the game was dreadful. The bus stopped at every pub on the way home and my teammates slowly drank themselves into oblivion while I waited alone on the bus. But I stayed with them, made a declaration of difference, developed a degree of detachment and put most of them to bed! It was a privilege! I was the alien half-back!

The second part of the price is that we are called to abstain from seductions. Peter wrote, "Dear friends, I urge you . . . to abstain from sinful desires, which war against your soul" (2:11). All of us are subject to external temptations and seductions to which we can easily respond through internal sinful desires. Being attacked on two fronts simultaneously can be overwhelming—the toxic mixing of seductions on the outside with sinful desires deeply embedded on the inside can lead to struggle and defeat, disappointment and despair. If we drop our guard we will be vulnerable to things that Peter rightly said "war against the soul!" Some of you have been in wars, you have smelled it, seen it, suffered from it. You have seen brave men die and innocent people suffer. You've watched as children were made orphans and neighborhoods were reduced to pitiful heaps of rubble. War is a beastly business.

When we give way to sinful desires, whether it be illicit sexual desires or appetites, anger or bitterness, jealousy, envy or any kind of hostility, opportunities to respond to these internal dynamics of our fallenness will be met by seductive opportunities to yield. At this point, war enters our souls. These things do as much damage to our souls as a tank driving through a plot of violets. Our lives, instead of being like the sweet countryside where the quiet rivers flow through meadows and slumbering villages, become like a battlefield littered with great craters full of muddy water, mechanical wreckage and the carnage of destroyed bodies. I'm not overdoing it because Peter uses these kinds of powerful words here.

Do you sometimes wonder why God seems so distant? Why is prayer such a bore to you and worship of no interest? Why is fellowship with God's people something you don't desire? Do you wonder why the sweet things of the Spirit sometimes feel totally foreign to you? It's because somewhere, somehow, under some circumstances, you succumbed to sinful desires within you because of the seductive influences outside you. They warred against your soul, and instead of the sweetness and the beauty of a spiritual life, there lies within you a barrenness; the bleakness of a battlefield. The price of privilege is to abstain in the power of the Spirit of God from those things which war against the soul. We can't do it on our own, but that's why God made us members of a "people" who will support us in the struggle. It's why God gave us His Spirit to equip us for the fight!

The price of privilege also means we must absorb the slander. The apostle Peter wrote, "Though they accuse you of doing wrong, they may see your good deeds and glorify God on the day he visits [you]" (2:12). The early Christians were subjected to all kinds of abuse and slander. Athenagorus, a Christian philosopher from Athens, wrote "A Plea for Christians" in A.D. 177 and addressed it to Marcus Aurelius and Lucius Aurelius, the Roman emperors. What he said in effect was that the Christians were getting a raw deal. They were being accused of all kinds of things and everybody was believing the accusations. The specific charges were that they were engaging in the practice of "Atheism, Thyestian Feasts and Oedinodean Intercourse."

Can you imagine the early Christians being accused of atheism by pagans? The pagans worshiped a multiplicity of gods and the believers refused to join them. Anybody who refused to worship the gods of the nation, national security and national prosperity, in pagan thinking, must be an atheist. In actual fact, Christians had discovered the true God and rejected the false gods. Nevertheless, they had to endure the ignominy of being accused by pagans of being what the pagans were themselves.

Then they were accused of attending Thyestian feasts. Thyestes was a man who organized banquets where the delicacy was human flesh. In other words, a Thyestian feast was a cannibalistic feast. The pagans accused the Christians of cannibalism. They had heard them quote the Lord Jesus, "Except you eat the flesh of the Son of Man and drink his blood, you have no life in you" (John 6:53). The pagans said, "You know what they do? They turn bread into flesh and wine into blood then eat and drink them. They are cannibals."

Not only that, they were accused of Oedipodean intercourse. In mythology, Oedipus was adopted as a child, grew up, saw a delightful lady, married her and found out eventually that he had married his mother. Freud gave them both a lot of publicity as he propagated his theories of sexual development, with particular reference to incestuous tendencies. But long before Freud, people were having trouble in this area, and the pagans were accusing the Christians of incestuous behavior. You see the Christians called all women "sisters." The men of the church had very close relationships with these "sisters" and actually married them. So the pagans, in their ignorance, put two and two together and came up with six.

When a Christian tries to live in an unchristian society he or she can be certain that just about everything stood for will be rejected, and much will be misinterpreted. We may well be slandered from beginning to end. So you know what we are to do? Absorb it! And how do we do that? By standing firm in our own conviction about the truth and waiting for the final judgment when God will reveal the secrets of men's hearts. And that's all part of the price of privilege.

The Practice of Privilege

Privileged people recognize that privilege brings opportunity as well as responsibility. We have the opportunity to "declare the praises of him who called [us] out of darkness into his wonderful light" (2:9). To be silent in the place of blessing is to fail in the seat of privilege. To say nothing of the virtues of God in the environment of His grace is to border on the insulting. It takes a conscious effort not to declare those things in which we delight; but to speak is as natural as to enjoy.

Secondly, we need to decline the vices of the society around us. In verse 12 Peter says, "Live such good lives among the pagans" and "among the pagans" is precisely where we live. We must not isolate ourselves. There is a great tendency for believers to pull out from society and to protect themselves from every outside influence. When we go to the extreme of Christian isolation from pagans, it is unbiblical and dangerous. It's dangerous for the Christian and disastrous for the pagan. Where do we live? We live among the pagans. How do we live? We live unlike the pagans. We live "good lives" among the pagans.

Thirdly, we begin to define the values of the world against us. Peter may be thinking back to the Sermon on the Mount when the Lord told His disciples that they were "salt" and "light" and that they were to let their "good works" be seen so that the observers might "glorify God" (see Matt. 5–7). In other words, the pagans are going to see the good deeds and recognize their goodness. But how are pagans going to recognize they are good if they have a different standard of values? The answer is straightforward: only when Christians begin to turn them from their ways instead of being turned around themselves. We have to define the values for the world. If they don't see Christian goodness, they will have no knowledge or experience of it.

There is a place for believers in the midst of a pagan society. That place is a challenging position of change and conflict fraught with problems and full of difficulties. For the fainthearted, this is threatening. For those secure in Christ, exciting.

10

THE CHRISTIAN CITIZEN
1 Peter 2:12–17

As Christians, we are citizens of heaven. Our permanent residence is there, but we live temporarily on earth. The way we live down here as citizens, recognizing the political, economic and sociological structures of the society in which we live, is very important. We're not just spiritual people living in a spiritual vacuum. Our true spirituality is demonstrated as we live in the midst of a secular society.

There are three particular areas of concern that Peter mentions which relate to our unique position in secular society: authority, liberty and dignity.

Authority and the Christian Citizen

Christians, of all people, understand and recognize the place of authority. We understand authority in principle because we believe in God—the Supreme Being from whom we come, through whom we survive and to whom we go. We believe we are answerable to Him because the very concept of God means that in Him ultimate authority resides. It is impossible to believe that God exists and not to believe in authority as a principle. Christians also believe that our world was created and it operates on discernible laws and principles. If this were not the case, science would be nonsense. But science assumes that there are discernible and predictable laws, and it is not surprising that early scientific endeavors were motivated by Christians who believed in laws, principles and authority.

Christians also believe that human beings are sinful and, because of this, authority is necessary in order that society might be made tolerable. C.S. Lewis said he was in favor of democracy, not because everybody is equally intelligent and equally qualified to have an equal say, but because everybody is equally sinful and we all need to keep an eye on each other! Christians recognize that all equally sinful people need principles of authority to keep us in check. Our belief presupposes belief in authority.

Christians also have good insights into the practice of authority. We recognize, as Peter says in verse 13, that authority has been instituted "for the Lord's sake" and it is to be submitted to because "it is God's will" (2:15). Paul, in Romans 13, develops this theme much more fully, explaining that authority is ordained of God. According to him there is no authority except that which God has established. Consequently, he who rebels against authority is rebelling against what God has instituted and will bring judgment on himself. We live in an antinomian age where people reject and resent authority. People are more concerned with individual freedoms and liberties than with being responsible members of society acknowledging the authorities. It is particularly important, therefore, that Christians maintain their special understanding of authority and show it in our lifestyles and behaviors.

Additionally, Christians recognize what authorities are supposed to do. Paul summarizes it very succinctly. He says that authorities are ordained to punish those who do wrong and to reward those who do right. One of the ways that Christian citizens live distinctively is by having a high view of authority and responding properly to it. That can mean accepting with grace rulings of those in authority with which we might not agree or, conversely, respectfully refusing to recognize authoritarian demands that contravene divine principle as Peter, himself, did when he was instructed by the authorities "not to speak or teach at all in the name of Jesus" (Acts 4:18).

The Christian's Response to Authority

The Christian response to authority is one of submission. There are three reasons for this. The first reason is because it is enjoined by God. Whether or not we agree with what God has said, He's said it. And whether or not we like what God has done, He's done it anyway. Our attitudes don't alter His edicts or his actions.

He has instituted authority structures made up of sinful humans, so they (the structures) are not perfect and will not always do what they are supposed to do. Nevertheless, Scripture teaches that God set people in authority and requires us to be submissive to them. Secondly, submission has been ingrained by the Holy Spirit. Remember in the first chapter of the epistle we were told to be "obedient children." We were shown that the work of the Trinity in our lives is designed to produce obedience. This whole concept of obedience runs through the pages of Spirit-inspired scripture and Spirit-taught principles. So whenever the Spirit works, He ingrains a healthy attitude toward obedience and authority. Thirdly, our Lord Jesus modeled submission. The very tone and fiber of His life on earth among us was one of acknowledging authority. Right at the end of His life He prayed, "My Father, if it is possible, may this cup be taken from me. Yet not as I will, but as you will" (Matt. 26:39). The cross was an acknowledging of the Father's final and ultimate authority. Christians, therefore, not only understand authority in principle and practice but develop submissive spirits and a willingness to respond to divinely ordained authority. But there is one big "but" here. There is another way of approaching the subject of authority as addressed by Peter and that is to measure what he did alongside what he said.

One day Peter was brought before the authorities. They interrogated him:

"Is it true that you have been preaching?"

"Yes."

"And is it true that you have been preaching in the name of Christ?"

"Yes."

"And is it true that we have forbidden you to do so?"

"Yes."

"Therefore you admit that, having been forbidden to preach in the name of Christ, you have been doing it?"

"Yes."

So Peter, the man who said, "submit to every authority" freely admitted that he had contravened his own rule! Was this gross insubordination or was there more to the situation than at first appears? Peter's problem was as old as the rocks of Galilee. Jesus commissioned his disciples to take the message of the gospel to the ends of the earth. But some authorities did not want this to happen and therefore forbade the disciples to do what Jesus had specifically instructed them to do! Jesus said one thing and the authorities ordained by God contradicted it. What were they to do? Peter's answer to the authorities was straightforward: "We must obey God rather than men" (Acts 5:29). Authorities instituted by God are there to reward those who do good and to punish those who do evil. It is there to maintain peace and order so that people may live productively and for God in a sinful society. But when the government itself becomes evil and opposes the good it is supposed to support, there is a major failure of authority and the Christian knows it. When the government actually contravenes the law of God and allows people to do what God has flatly forbidden, the Christian recognizes that the ultimate authority is God's. And civil disobedience may be necessary and, in some cases, even mandatory!

We must be very careful at this point because popular attitudes at the present time encourage insubordination. It is normal to answer the referee back, to downgrade authority figures, to evade taxes, to rebel against parents. Peter's principle must not be regarded as an excuse for insubordination. It is a simple escape clause to be used only when there is a clear conflict between what God has said and what divinely ordained authority tells us to do or allows to happen. A young woman came to me and said, "I've become a Christian and the Bible says I should submit to my husband as the one who is the authority in my family. My husband is opposed to Christianity but he keeps reminding me that Christian wives submit to authority—and he sees himself as my authority. He told me that he wanted me to go to a wife swapping party with him, but I didn't want to go. But he told me to submit to his authority! I talked to some Christian friends and they said I should obey, that they would pray and God would deliver me. But when I found myself in bed with somebody else's husband I realized that God didn't deliver me." What a tragedy that her well-meaning friends had such an inadequate understanding of the biblical teaching on submission to authority!

Liberty and the Christian Citizen

With superb balance Peter commands, "Live as free people, but do not use your freedom as a cover-up for evil; live as servants of God" (2:16). Living like free men is a very popular subject in our day. It shows itself in moral standards, political stances and personal priorities. The common desire appears to be that there should be no restrictions that way we can enjoy what we fondly imagine to be liberty. We don't seem to understand that to take away limits and restrictions does not produce liberty; it simply promotes anarchy. But there is another kind of freedom. This freedom does not focus on demolishing restrictions but on the recognition of hindrances and habits that inhibit a person's ability to live well. A teenager given an hour's extension to his curfew time may rejoice in that newfound freedom but if he uses it to indulge a growing dependency on drugs, he can hardly claim to be free.

To understand liberty properly as Christians we must first look into the law of liberty (see James 1:25). This expression appears to couple two mutually contradictory terms—law and liberty. But, contrary to many heady theories, we must recognize that if we're going to be free we must come under the law (or principle) of freedom that is contained in the Word of God. This means, among other things, that we recognize Christ the Lord as Liberator, Redeemer and Savior from the consequences and dominion of sin; even our habits or addictions.

It is in the deliverance of Christ that there is freedom but it is under His lordship that His freedom is offered. He gives freedom from things that hinder and mar and spoil us as individuals, things that wreck us as a society. But this freedom is given only according to the principles of God's Word. Christians know this and refuse to be taken in by all the talk about individual rights to do whatever we wish. We look into all movements—whether freedom, liberation, revolutionary or reactionary—through the filter of God's Word. Therein, and only therein, do we discover the perfect law of liberty that allows real freedom.

Secondly, Christians recognize the limits of liberty because we know that human beings were created to be dependent and interdependent. Dependency and interdependency are clearly God-ordained limits upon our human liberty. We are free to breathe but not without air, to feed but not without food, to relate but not without relationships. All this is determined by God and there is no escaping His limits. Liberty, therefore, is found not in the absence of limits but in living joyfully and freely and submissively within God-ordained limits.

Thirdly, we need to recognize the nature of the life of liberty. Peter says we are not to "use [our] freedom as a cover-up for evil; [but to] live as servants of God" (2:16). Isn't it interesting that the words *servant* (or *slave*) and *liberty* appear in the same context? He is telling us that our liberty is exercised properly when we freely submit ourselves to His lordship, freely commit ourselves to His service, and freely accept the role of a disciple. When this is done, we know the truth of Jesus' words, if you "know the truth . . . the truth will set you free" (John 8:32). A look into the perfect law of liberty reveals that liberty has its limits and that true liberty is found in submission to the Lord Jesus and acceptance of a life of discipleship and service. The abuse of liberty produces excesses of liberty. That is why, again, Peter warns that we must not use our liberty "as a cover-up (or cloak) for evil." It's very easy to say, "I'm free so I can do what I like." without realizing that "what I like" is fleshly and sinful and, therefore, my freedom talk has become a cover for evil actions. Economic liberty can produce the evil of greed, political liberty the evil of pride and religious liberty the evil of license. Liberty can also be an excuse for laziness. I often pass through Miami airport, pushing my way through thousands of people from all over South and Central America and North America. But among the crowds I always see people I know, no matter what time of day or night.

There is a girl there who is about 6'2". There is a little pimply youth with a hairpiece. They sell books, they give away flowers and expect a donation. They have blank eyes and are members of a cult! They are trying to earn their salvation. That's why they are there and that's why they work day and night! Now evangelical Christians know salvation is a gift and is not a reward for a job well done or a life well lived.

We know that Ephesians 2:8–9 tells us that we are saved by grace through faith and not by works of righteousness. We are "free from works" as a means of salvation, but unfortunately, compared to cults, we often use our liberty as an excuse for spiritual laziness. What then is the exercise of liberty? Peter tells us quite simply to "Live as servants of God" (2:16) which means, freely choose a life of service. In freely choosing the life of service, we clearly show submission to the One we belong to and whom we serve. The pagans may then inquire as we serve God, "Do you have to do that?"

"No."

"Well, why do you do it?"

"Because I serve the living God and in His name I commit myself to you."

That's why being a volunteer in the service of Jesus Christ is so challenging to a selfish person. That is why we need to underline the absolute necessity of using our liberty freely to do acts of service to the living God and to mankind.

Dignity and the Christian Citizen

"Show proper respect to everyone: Love the brotherhood of believers, fear God, honor the king" (2:17), says the apostle Peter. To treat a person with dignity means to regard them, respect them and honor them because they deserve to be so treated. We may feel that some people are less deserving of respect and honor than others but the Christian has a unique way of approaching the subject of dignity.

Christians should treat all individuals with dignity and respect. Not necessarily because they are high achievers or social benefactors but because God does! Every individual was created by God! Christ died for him and God has eternal plans for her. It is hard to imagine how God could show any more clearly his high regard for the creatures he made and the eternal significance with which he has invested them. And all of this applies to the person who would probably be disregarded by some and perhaps even abused as being of little significance by people who miss the spiritual realities of a person's being. No one should have a higher view of the worth of an individual than a well-versed Christian believer.

Christians should respect the brotherhood of believers. Not all gatherings are known for their dignified behavior and it is not always the case that the people involved are regarded with respect. But the brotherhood of believers is different. They are a group who has recognized their need of a Savior and have come in repentance and faith to Christ, developing a new lifestyle together that seeks to model what Christ taught his disciples. They are willing to serve, sacrifice their time and talents and invest in worthy causes.

They deserve respect and frequently receive it. Christians must have a tremendous sense of the dignity of the Lord Himself. It is summarized in Peter's term "fear God" (2:17). We know that from Him we come and to Him we go and through Him and for Him we exist. Without God, we are nothing and have nothing so we have a great sense of His majesty. We come into His presence with a great sense of His awesome dignity. *Awesome* is a word that has lost much of its powerful meaning. The word Peter used means to be taken aback by something so startling that you stop dead in your tracks and take a step backwards to recover. That's awe! Because we focus (rightly so) on God's grace does not mean that we should neglect the balancing truth of God's majesty and power. In fact we may even need to ponder the following words from Hebrews 12:28, "Let us be thankful and so worship God acceptably with reverence and awe, for our God is a consuming fire."

Christians "honor the king" or at least they were called to do so in the days of the Roman emperors. Many believers today live in nations that no longer honor royalty. Yet they do live in structures of government where people of responsibility are called to care for the wellbeing of the people. As many of these influential people are also political figures, this almost guarantees that they will be warmly supported by some and reviled by others. Christians are often caught up in this sad modern phenomenon called the political landscape. But because we recognize that authority structures are ordained by God (see Rom. 13) as a means of delegating divine authority for the wellbeing of the people, Christians are called to treat public officials who serve the people with the respect they deserve—even if they will not vote for them!!

Christians have a long tradition of recognizing the dignity of the poor, the underprivileged and the oppressed. Despite these individual's deprivation, they are human. They are children of God, made in His image, redeemable and precious in His eyes. God's people see the least and the lost as spiritual, physical and social beings whose fallenness is manifested in all areas of their lives. With great compassion and grace we go out to those in the favelas of Latin America, the Dalits in their untouchable villages and slums in India, the displaced refugees all over the Middle East and anywhere and everywhere else where the poor and the oppressed are to be found.

Respect for "the brotherhood of believers" (2:17) is not always apparent as modern churches spend more time and effort competing with each other rather than complementing and complimenting each other. A young man, not yet a follower of Jesus, asked me recently why there are many denominations among Christians and why they do not seem to get along with each other. It was a penetrating question that requires heart searching for many of us as we consider what it means to treat even our brothers and sisters in Christ with respect and dignity.

Respect for the Lord seems to be out of place in this list of those to whom respect is due. Surely honoring the Lord is a "given" and yet Peter does include "fear God" (2:17). It means we reverence Him. We must have a high regard for Him. We must take Him seriously and take to heart what He says. We seek to bring our lives into line with what He has commanded, living gladly in terms of what He has promised. You could say that not doing so is disrespectful—and that is putting it mildly!

I recently read about a seventeenth-century German theologian and pastor named Herman August Franck. Pastor Franck had such a concern for the preaching of Christ to the underprivileged and poor that he built orphanages, schools and homes for the wayward and lost. He was deeply involved in the lives of these people and, in the name of Christ, he sought to treat them with dignity. He loved the brotherhood of believers and was deeply involved in the authority structures of his society. Above all, he feared God and served the Lord Jesus. Eventually all the institutions he founded and all the ministries he initiated fell into the hands of the Communists when his country became part of the godless Soviet Empire. But the esteem in which he was held was such that they preserved his work. They paid for the upkeep of his library and they maintained his buildings. While they rejected his God and refused to bow a knee to his Lord, they did not and would not deny what Pastor Franck did. His Christian commitment exuded dignity and all who came within the sphere of his influence were treated with grace, respect and dignity.

If you go to (East) Germany and see what is left of the ministry of Herman August Franck, you'll see a remarkable tribute to a man who understood authority, liberty and dignity. It is a tribute that lives on in the midst of a pagan society two or three centuries after his death. He proved that Peter was right when he said, "By doing good [we] should silence the ignorant talk of foolish men" (2:15). The word *silence* in this passage is translated as "to muzzle a yapping dog." We're called to be spiritual in a secular world. We are citizens of heaven living down here in this world. We're called to be servants and disciples of the living Christ in a world that is fundamentally pagan. And in living as we're called to, in the power of the Spirit, we put to silence the criticisms of those who don't know the Lord we proclaim. This creates an opportunity to speak of the grace they so desperately need.

11

INJUSTICE
1 Peter 2:18–25

It is probable that a high percentage of early Christians were slaves. We have an understandable and natural abhorrence for the institution of slavery, and we thank God that it was overthrown and that ultimately the Christian church dealt with this structured assault on human dignity. The Lord Jesus said practically nothing about slavery and His disciples were no more vocal than He, but that does not mean that they were not doing something about it. It has been estimated that there were approximately 870,000 people living in Rome around the beginning of the first century and, in a thirty-year period, 500,000 of those 870,000 people were slaves who gained their freedom. Imagine what would happen to a society if suddenly a sizeable piece of the population is "let go." They are homeless, jobless and resourceless. They are dumped on a society with no way of caring for them or even of allowing them to care for themselves! That is a picture of the slavery situation in New Testament times.

Maybe that is part of the reason why the politically powerless, early Christians apparently made no attempt to overthrow the system. Yet there was certainly a deep commitment to the apostolic teaching in the life of the early believers. Teaching that ministered to both slaves and slave owners so that relationships and living conditions could change dramatically

Christian teaching on the subject of slaves, slave owners, mistreatment and injustice is not without relevance today. Stories abound of Christians being unjustly imprisoned. We have friends who have suffered terribly in Iranian prisons. We have met with and prayed for pastors formerly imprisoned in China, Myanmar and Siberia. The horrors of human trafficking have become increasingly clear to us as one of our "granddaughters" has moved into the Red Light district of Bangkok, Thailand to reach out to the men and women responsible for and caught up in the iniquitous sex trade. Injustice abounds in today's world.

But there is no doubt it requires a stretch of the imagination to bridge the gap between life for slaves and freemen of the first century and for most of us who live in the twenty-first century. Nevertheless, some of us, perhaps, think we're slaves to kitchen sinks or we're the property of uncaring and demanding employers, and we need to know how to handle what we perceive as a grave injustice—or at least less than ideal working conditions!

Injustice and the Extreme of Slavery

In the New Testament, a slave was simply treated as property. His feelings, his rights and his personhood were of little concern. He was regarded as a unit of production, a piece of property, beef, brawn and muscle. He was the means of getting a job done rather than a person of eternal consequence. Aristotle, who said many enlightened things, was well below his best when he said, "Masters and slaves have nothing in common; a slave is simply a living tool."

We may wonder how people became slaves. A high percentage of them were, of course, born in slavery. Many of them were prisoners of war who had been captured in overseas campaigns. Some of them had gotten into such financial straits that their only resources were the lives of their wives, children and selves. When they went bankrupt, they sold themselves as slaves to creditors. (This practice was banned in Rome in 326 BC). Then there were those who were actually bred as slaves. Their parents had been "mated" by unscrupulous owners. This kind of slavery was common at the time of Peter was writing.

However, there was a brighter side to the situation. Many slaves were being granted their freedom, but not always for altruistic reasons! The Romans had a problem manning their armies, and when they couldn't get volunteers, they released slaves and immediately drafted them. Talk about out of the frying pan into the fire! Just prior to Peter's time of writing, half a million slaves had been released to Rome itself, many of them had been sent off to the colonies against their desires. When the Romans wanted to colonize an area and nobody wanted to go, they simply released the slaves and made them establish the new colonies. Some gained their freedom when the master died. Taxes were based on the number of people in the household, and some owners didn't want to pay taxes on old worn-out slaves, so they kicked them out. Terrible injustice was the lot of a high percentage of the populace in Peter's day, and the problem was real in the small congregations of believers.

Slavery was accepted under certain circumstances in Israel in Old Testament times, but it was regulated by very strict rules. Hebrews could not own a Hebrew slave. They could have people from other countries as slaves but they had to release them on the seventh year. Then, of course, there was the great year of Jubilee, which was especially important for slaves. The beautiful Liberty Bell in Philadelphia bears the inscription, "Proclaim liberty throughout the land." That is a superb example of taking a verse out of its context and making it say exactly what it isn't saying.

That quotation has nothing to do with the American Revolution or the French Revolution. It comes from Leviticus 25 which explains that on the fiftieth year, the year of Jubilee, all slaves were to be liberated. This was certainly not what many of the founding fathers had in mind in Philadelphia! So some slaves in ancient Israel had more grounds for hope than those who lived in colonial and revolutionary America, despite what the Liberty Bell says.

When we get into the early Christian church scene, we find that Peter was writing to many people who were slaves, former slaves or masters of slaves. He doesn't say to the slaves, "revolt and run away," and he doesn't say to the masters, "let them go." He tells them to start regarding each other as people of infinite worth and, therefore, build each other up, care for each other and love each other! We all know that the system of slavery could not survive this revolutionary approach. In this way, Christianity laid an axe at the root of the tree of slavery. It was by a careful, invisible revolution of love, nurture and care that people's attitudes were changed and society was rid of a blot on her countenance. This is a powerful message for us today. The ideal situation would be where both slave and owner acted Christianly to each other while working toward a solution for the social ill in which they were both trapped. But many slaves lived in grossly unjust situations, and to them Peter wrote, "Submit yourselves to your masters with all respect, not only to those who are good and considerate, but also to those who are harsh" (2:18).

We can apply this to our situation and remind ourselves that the Christian approaches to injustice are quite different from other people's. Peter says, categorically, "To this you were called" (2:21). To what? The previous sentence tells us. He writes, "If you suffer for doing good and you endure it, this is commendable before God. To this you were called." The Christian attitude toward injustice means he will accept what is coming to him in all good conscience because he realizes that he was "called" to this kind of behavior. This remarkable statement is undergirded by the example of the Savior in His reaction to injustice. "Christ suffered for you, leaving you an example, that you should follow in his steps" (2:21). This verse has often been taken out of context and applied to all kinds of things, but its real significance is that it gives an example of how a Christian handles injustice.

Many years ago, during the Cold War, I read the biography of a Russian Jew who was imprisoned in Moscow after his wife had been deported to Israel. He was subjected to all kinds of abuse and deprivation over an extended period during which time he developed a hard unrelenting hatred for his abusers. He became a broken desperate man but in the quiet darkness of solitary confinement he realized that his hatred was adding to his own suffering and doing nothing to alleviate his situation. So he looked for an alternative and began to focus on the man who was causing his suffering rather than the suffering he was being subjected to. He tried to imagine the life of this hard cruel person. He focused on the needs of this man and gradually the prisoner's attitudes changed and hatred turned to pity, anger to concern. It is hard for us to imagine life under such circumstances but I find them helpful as a reminder of the enormity of the patient suffering of our Lord and the example that He gives us as His followers.

Injustice and the Example of the Savior

Jesus was subjected to a Hebrew trial before the Sanhedrin and a Roman trial before Pontius Palate. Sanhedrin trials were designed to ensure that justice be done but Jesus' trial before the Sanhedrin was riddled with irregularities. Sanhedrin trials were supposed to start with statements for the acquittal of the accused. Sometimes the evidence for acquittal was so compelling that the prosecution would not be presented. In the case of the Lord Jesus, there was not even a word as to why He should be acquitted. In fact, he was captured and taken before the Sanhedrin by people who were intent on having Him put to death. Not only that, the trial was illegal because the Sanhedrin was not allowed to meet on the Sabbath or on a feast day. But Christ was tried on Passover. Capital offenses could not be tried at night, and the death penalty could not be passed until the day following the trial. Yet Christ was sentenced to death at a night trial. The Roman trial was equally a travesty of justice.

Jesus' accusers took Him to the Roman governor because he alone had the right to pass the death penalty. In the Sanhedrin, they charged Him with blasphemy, but before Pilate, the charge was altered to treason. When Pilate examined Him under that charge he said, "I find no fault in this man" (Luke 23:4). In other words, He was acquitted. At that moment, Jesus should have been allowed to go free. But the judge succumbed to the threats of the crowd. He washed his hands of the whole matter knowing he was sending an innocent man to death.

Peter, writing to slaves, reminds them that their Savior lived and died in an unjust world and handled it well. When they hurled insults at Him, He did not retaliate. When He suffered, He made no threats. He responded to the situation uniquely, and Peter's thrust is that those who suffer injustice as Christians are to follow His example.

Also, there was inhumanity in Jesus' death on the cross. Crucifixion was not a Jewish means of execution but a Roman invention. It is interesting that Jews were particularly anxious to have Him crucified. No doubt the leaders of His opposition wanted Him to have the most humiliating death imaginable. Crucifixion to a Jew would bring the ultimate shame because the Old Testament said, "Cursed is everyone who hangs on a tree" (see Gal. 3:13; Deut. 21:23). And if Jesus died cursed on a cross, no one would ever believe that He was the Messiah because surely the Messiah was not cursed (they had not grasped Isaiah 53)! That's what they wanted for Him, the ultimate shame and degradation and the final burying of any Messianic beliefs and aspirations.

As He hung in shame, He was confronted with the undisguised hostility of the crowds that had gathered around. They mocked and jeered at Him, intent on adding agony to ignominy. Even one who was crucified at His side turned on Him and vilified Him. His disciples had forsaken Him and fled, and as He looked up to the Father He cried from the depth of His soul, "My God, my God, why have you forsaken me?" (Matt. 27:46). All this, Peter says, portrayed the awful injustice to which Christ was subjected.

There is great significance in Christ's example. Instead of taking matters into His own hands, He entrusted them into God's hands. Peter says, "When he suffered, he made no threats. Instead, he entrusted himself to him who judges justly" (2:23). When we suffer injustice we need to resist the natural impulse to take matters into our own hands and we must commend ourselves to the keeping of the One who judges justly. We also need to notice that Jesus endured on behalf of other people. In fact, it says in verse 21, "Christ suffered for you." Some people think that Christ was just suffering for His own actions or because of Pilate's cowardice or because of the hostility of the leaders of His day. But the Bible teaches that God foreordained the sufferings of Christ before the foundation of the world. If He had taken matters into His own hands when He was subjected to injustice, He might have preserved His own position, but He would have disqualified Himself from being the means of blessing to everybody on the face of God's earth. He endured the injustice to bring blessing to others. Christ was also prepared to endure the injustice because Peter tells us, "By his wounds you have been healed" (2:24). In His act of submission to injustice, there was potential healing for the very people who subjected Him to the injustice! As they crucified Him, He prayed: "Father, forgive them, for they do not know what they are doing" (Luke 23:34). In the illegality of His trials, He did not complain about injustice and in the inhumanity of His cross, He did not retaliate against the ignominy. But He committed His affairs into the hand of God as He looked upon the concerns of others. He knew that the wounds in His own body would bring healing to many.

"To this you were called" and "this being the example of our Lord" says the apostle to the slaves in the churches. Not that he minimized the injustice of the slaves' situation. He didn't approve of it and he didn't agree with it, but he encouraged them to handle injustice properly. In the end, justice would be done and innumerable people would be blessed.

Injustice and the Experience of the Shepherd

We now need to consider practically how these powerful truths about the Christian response to injustice should be handled. We should recognize the root of injustice. Peter points out that Christ, as He was suffering under injustice, was dealing with sins. So let's start by calling injustice by its proper name—sin. I'm not just quoting the Bible at this moment. I'm also quoting good old Abraham Lincoln. In 1854

he said, "Slavery is grounded in the selfishness of man's nature, opposition to it in his love of justice." Lincoln saw in
injustice the selfishness of man's nature and Peter saw the
sinfulness of man's nature. A Christian does not discard a
sinner like a rotten apple—selfish to the core. We approach
a sinner as a person for whom Christ died. And this applies
to our response to perpetrators of injustice. If we regard injustice as the product of people we despise and hate, we will
retaliate and produce conflict. If we, as Christians, regard
injustice as the product of the sinful nature, we will call the
unjust sinners and take steps to express concern for them.
Slaves should submit to masters who treat them badly because their masters are proving they are sinners by their
unjust actions; and slaves have been known to lead sinful
masters to repentance!

We need to return to the Shepherd. Peter says, "You were
like sheep going astray, but now you have returned to the
Shepherd and Overseer of your souls" (2:25). God chose,
of all the animals in creation, to call human beings "sheep."
He could have compared us to strong oxen or noble horses or even cute kittens, but He preferred to call us sheep.
Sheep have an inbuilt waywardness, a remarkable capacity
for going wrong. When left to their own devices, sheep will
foul things up. But when given a shepherd, it's amazing how
they change! Our world is full of injustice because wayward
sheep, doing their own thing, have rejected the Shepherd.
Our society is suffering because it is made up of people who
disregard the Shepherd's leading and are heaping injustice
upon injustice and producing retaliation against retaliation. But in the midst of it, there are some people who have

chosen to return to the Shepherd, to reject waywardness and to commit themselves to the Overseer of their souls. When the Overseer, our Example, takes over, His impetus begins to produce reactions to injustice similar to His own.

We need to respond to the call. As we have seen, Peter reminds believers of their call—not to mediocrity or to conformity, but to uniqueness and submissiveness. This idea of "calling" was powerful in Peter's thinking because it was only because of God's "call" that he was an apostle and not a fisherman; a winner of the souls of men rather than a fisher of the denizens of the deep. Equally powerful to him was the calling to distinctive behavior in the teeth of injustice.

We need to relate to the cross. Peter wrote, "He himself bore our sins in his body on the tree [not simply in order that we might have our sins forgiven and live happily ever after, but] so that we might die to sins and live for righteousness" (2:24).

Look at it this way. When Jesus died on the cross, He showed His true feelings about sin. Those feelings contrast sharply with our tendency to take sin lightly once sins have been forgiven. Peter insists that when we identify with the Lord Jesus, we adopt His attitude toward sin. We die to what He died to and live for what He lives for. Our retaliation against injustice might be as sinful as the injustice imposed upon us in the first place. Once we are conscious of its sinfulness and our stance on sin, our lives must be committed to a new view of injustice in all its forms. To follow the example of Christ when faced with injustice must not become a noble, empty phrase or a futile soul-destroying exercise. The only way I know to avoid both extremes is to bear in mind continually that He is not only Example, but also Enabler. I once took my small children to play in a field of new snow. I ran around in a circle taking giants strides and told them to follow my example. They failed, of course. Their little legs were far too short. So I placed my hands under their armpits, their feet on mine, and together we made giant strides. In a sense, they discovered my abilities flowing through them, to their intense delight. I know of nothing more delightful than reacting uniquely as Christ did because He showed me that I ought to, and shows me, through His power, that I can.

12

MARRIAGE IN FOCUS

1 Peter 3:1–7

The words of an old song from my youth frequently come to mind in my pastoral counseling. The lyrics are, "We always hurt the ones we love, the ones we shouldn't hurt at all." And I must admit that I have been guilty of such behavior on occasion. When we are under pressure, we lash out at people in frustration, and frequently the people on the receiving end are the people closest at hand. Perhaps we know we can do this because we've done it before and we were forgiven and got away with it! But over time our interpersonal relationships suffer and if we are not careful they disintegrate. This is particularly tragic because the relationships we destroy at such times are designed to be a source of great strength, not the scene of great conflict.

God ordained marriage for the well-being of both the individual and society. A solid, stable marriage can and should be a tremendous resource in difficult times. But it is a sad commentary on our society today that marriages are fracturing under stress instead of nourishing those who find life difficult. It is important to note that Peter takes time to write about marriage in the context of his concern for believers living in the end times. The disciples were no doubt aware that Jesus surprised people by saying "At the resurrection people will neither marry nor be given in marriage. They will be like the angels in heaven" (Matt. 22:30). Peter and his friends might have concluded that marriage, therefore, was not high on Jesus' list of priorities. But this teaching from Peter clearly shows that marriage was still very much part of the divine order of things and in difficult times there are few more stabilizing factors than a solid marriage relationship. He spoke at length on the subject and showed that as submission is an integral part of the believer's lifestyle, so submission is a powerful factor in the development of a healthy marriage. Peter started out his teaching by stating, "Wives in the same way be submissive to your husbands" (3:1) and "Husbands in the same way be considerate as you live with your wives and treat them with respect" (3:7).

Applying the Principles of Christian Marriage

Sound marriages that survive stress, like solid buildings, are built on firm foundations—God given principles.

The first principle to consider is that of spiritual equality. Husband and wives should see that we are heirs together. Peter wrote that husbands should regard their wives as "heirs with you of the gracious gift of life" (3:7). Paul went even further when he wrote, "Now if we are children, then we are heirs—heirs of God and co-heirs with Christ if indeed we share in his sufferings in order that we may share in his glory" (Romans 8:17). We are heirs to all that Christ is heir to which means one day we will share the glory of

God and will live for all eternity in the presence of the living God! The men of Paul and Peter's era probably thought that was wonderful and exciting news, but apparently they needed to be reminded that their wives were just as much heirs! They were heirs together.

Husbands and wives are heirs together of the grace of God. Paul said, "By the grace of God I am what I am" (1 Cor. 15:10). This suggests that if there was anything of significance, anything of importance, anything of relevance in his life, it was attributable to the undeserved intervention of God. Peter insists that husbands see their wives in a similar light, as inheritors of God's grace.

Men, we are also heirs of life, not just life down here, but life eternal. Both husband and wife share this exalted position—a life of eternal and spiritual equality. Christian marriage rests on the solid basis of spiritual equality. Two people who are heirs of God and joint heirs with Christ, with identical eternal expectations, attributing everything to the grace of God, having become recipients of life eternal and sharing their lives—that's the firm foundation! In the days in which Peter was writing, women were still regarded as property, little better than slaves. The New Testament teaching on the place of women must be seen in this context, and we will realize what a positive, liberating effect the gospel had on the women and what joy it could bring to their marriages. By insisting that men see who women are "in Christ," marriage was elevated into a new and glorious position, which we must affirm in our day.

The principle of spiritual equality requires married couples to say our prayers together. Peter tells his readers to live as joint heirs "so that nothing will hinder your prayers" (3:7). He assumes that they both believe in prayer because they both believe that God rules in their affairs. They both relate to Him all their concerns and problems and plans. They both pray about their children, finances, jobs, homes and futures. But the warning is clear: if there is not a partnership base to a marriage and they are not praying together as joint heirs would be expected to pray, then their praying might be seriously hindered. Prayer is also an indication of gratitude. People who pray are people who praise. People who praise are people who understand the grace of God and respond to it in gratitude. A grateful spirit and a praising heart will counter the bickering and fighting that too often pervade the atmosphere of a stress-filled marriage.

We must also share our cares together. This is a beautiful aspect of togetherness. God, having created man, decided it was not good for man to be alone so He made woman. By bringing woman into man's life, He introduced an immediate and unique resource—what the old Bibles call "a helpmeet." She was somebody who would be utterly supportive and totally ideal for the situation. Standing by her man, standing alongside him through thick and thin, she would be what he could never be and do what he could never do. And while she was supporting and encouraging him, he was doing the same for her; sharing and caring for each other, together. Many couples don't need to get into a lot of marriage counseling. All they need to do is introduce these aspects of spiritual equality into their relationship.

The second principle to consider is sexual mutuality or mutual comfort. Peter writes, "Husbands, in the same way be considerate as you live with your wives" (3:7). The Greek word for "live with your wives" is most interesting. In contemporary English, we sometimes talk about people "living together" but what we mean is that they share the same bed without the commitment to marriage. Peter's word has a similar emphasis and in using the term, "living together" refers to sexual mutuality, the sharing of bodies, an integral part of marriage. This principle must be carefully built into marriage because it is an exercise in mutuality. *Together* is the most important word here. When we come together, sexually or otherwise, we can reasonably expect mutual comfort. A man in trouble at the office, if he has built his marriage properly, can come home and instead of being nagged, he will be comforted. But at the same time, his wife who has had a horrendous day can reasonably expect some understanding and support too. It is no accident that the gentle concern of a woman can best calm a frantic husband and the solid support of a man can best strengthen a woman who is sinking under life's stresses.

The principle of sexual mutuality also includes mutual companionship. Marriage partners must be good friends who enjoy each other's company. My wife and I, after fifty-eight years of marriage, are better friends than we have ever been. We both travel extensively; frequently together but often independently. I remember one trip where I visited exotic places like Guatemala, Hong Kong, Hawaii and the Bahamas but when Jill picked me up at the airport, we went out and leisurely ate a pizza and talked! That pizza, frankly, was the highlight of the trip because it was an experience of mutual comfort and mutual companionship.

There is also mutual completion. Men who I have met previously sometimes introduce the beautiful lady standing beside them as, "This is Linda, my better half." And some men even go on to say, "As you can see, I married up!" There is a very real possibility that both of these statements contain a great deal of truth but they are usually said in a jocular manner and elicit polite laughter. But what if they were true statements? The woman in question has qualities that the man lacks and her standing in society is more appropriate than his? For the man to recognize this and to admit it seriously would be to affirm the wife and prompt the "lesser half" to serious life change given the wife's example. Both men and women need to admit that there are great gaping holes in their marital experience and recognize God brought forth a man or woman to complete what is lacking in the other. You might be saying, "I thought this section was about sexual mutuality! When are you going to talk about it?" In fact, I have been talking about it but it is imperative that we see that sexuality is not just about the coupling of bodies but is intimately related to the comforting of spirits, the companionship of persons and the completion of whole personalities.

One of the great tragedies of our contemporary society is that we have divorced the giving of bodies in the sex act from the giving of ourselves in mutuality. We have divorced the physical and sexual from the reality of the psychological and the spiritual, and have brought untold disaster into our society. In a healthy marriage, there will be a "living together" in the fullest sense of the word. Sexuality brings mutual comfort, demonstrates mutual companionship and develops mutual completion in a unique way. It is absolutely fundamental that it be there, and much of the responsibility to see that these qualities exist in a marriage rests firmly with the husband's "being considerate" in this particularly precious and sensitive area of marriage.

Bearing in mind the prevailing attitudes of men about women at the time, we can see in Peter's epistle the uplifting impact the Christian message had on first century society. It goes without saying that the twenty-first century will need a similar uplifting if the contemporary erosion of human sexuality and marriage continues.

One extreme we have in our society is that there are people who want their sex without marriage. On the other hand, there are those who would like marriage without sex. Neither will do, for true mutuality is a sharing of the whole person with a whole person.

The next principle I'd like to note is physical disparity. Returning to verse 7 we read, "Husbands . . . live with your wives, and treat them with respect as the weaker partner." In our modern society, where women are standing up and being counted, the fur begins to fly when the "weaker partner" is introduced. There is no suggestion in Scripture that the woman is spiritually inferior. She is spiritually equal as we have seen. Those of us who have been to school should know that women are definitely not intellectually inferior. Women are most definitely not morally inferior. In fact, when it comes down to moral issues women often have a keener sense of what is right than men. And when it comes to sheer courage, my observation as a pastor is that when there are problems in marriage, 95 percent of the time it's the women who have the courage to deal with it. Men are less likely to do so. So when we talk about women being the "weaker partner," I believe we're talking about physical limitations. No doubt I will be challenged to run a marathon now by some of the girls who have done it, or challenged as I was recently by a beautiful young female athlete to put the shot. There are certainly exceptions to this rule. But it is generally true despite specific exceptions. This means that a husband must build in the principle of physical disparity and demonstrate it with a sensitivity to his wife's physical limitations. There also needs to be an awareness of the emotional pressures that those physical limitations bring. Many marriages experience difficulties because the wife is expected to run the home, raise the kids, hold down a job, look like a dream, be a gourmet cook and perform like a sexual gymnast. Christian men, particularly, need to build into their marriages an understanding of physical disparity, and treat their wives accordingly.

One day Peter said to the Lord, "We have left everything to follow you . . . what then will there be for us?" This was Peter at his feistiest! The Lord replied, "Everyone who has left houses or brothers or sisters or father or mother or children or fields for my sake will receive a hundred times as much and will inherit eternal life" (Matt. 19:27–29). In short, the Lord Jesus told Peter that being a disciple would make great demands on his home life, marriage and children. The early church was founded by men and women who understood and accepted this worthy call of discipleship. However, in First Corinthians 9, Paul, talking about the rights of an apostle, claimed he had as much right to take a wife on his journeys as Peter. In the early days of ministry, Peter's call meant he had to go away from home and live apart from his wife and family for periods of time. Later on, he obviously took his wife with him. We are not told why there was a change in the arrangement but it is obvious that either way, marriage is a challenge, discipleship is challenging and doing both at the same time is more challenging and requires the grace that is available in Christ.

There is also the principle of practical authority. I have dealt at some length with the latter part of this section of Scripture because I feel that, in our society, where there is an abundance of Christian teaching on marriage, there is often an inordinate emphasis on the woman's role in reference to her submission. Having taken time to talk about the man's role, I feel it's safe now to go to verse 1 that reads "Wives, in the same way be submissive to your husbands" (3:1). As we have seen, the Christian in all areas of his experience, recognizes authority. We understand submission because we acknowledge Christ as Lord. Bearing all this in mind, Peter instructs wives to demonstrate this attitude to their husbands—hence the introductory "in the same way."

Authority structures are necessary in all areas of society including marriage. We have noted that male and female have equality, enjoy mutuality and recognize disparity. But everyone knows that when groups of more than one person live in equality not everybody can make the necessary decisions. So when decisions have to be made, somebody must take charge. The buck has to stop somewhere. And God says in marriage the buck stops with the male, who has authority over the female. Some wives will claim that they are better at making decisions than their man. That may well be true. But they should remember that their decisiveness led them to an indecisive husband, so maybe they are not so good at deciding after all!

Seriously, when there is genuine equality of male and female, when a decision has to be made, there will be mutual sharing and double impact. And on the rare occasions that agreement is not reached, the man must decide and the woman must submit to the decision. In my marriage, I remember only three occasions when I had to "put my foot down." Jill says four, but I conveniently forget the fourth because I was wrong! Where there is mutuality, there is a pulling together, a building up together and a mutual giving to each other, so decisions will usually be unanimous. When they aren't, and somebody has to make an awkward decision, the other person will be supportive because equality and mutuality are the basis of marriage. These are the principles that must be built into Christian marriages. Men have the special responsibility to see that they are in operation.

On reading this section of the epistle, it would be easy to assume that women need six times as much instruction as men, because he addresses six verses to wives and only one to husbands. This was not the case! In the early days of the church, it was not uncommon for a pagan woman to become a Christian without her husband making a similar commitment. But if the man became a believer, he would require, as head of the family, that the wife join him in the faith. It was not unusual to find a marriage between a pagan man and a Christian woman, but it most unlikely to find one between a pagan woman and a Christian man.

These early Christians, as we have seen, were confronting tough times when Peter wrote to them, and he was eager to point out the great resource of a Christian marriage. But such a resource was not available to the Christian partner in a mixed marriage, so Peter has detailed instructions for them. He makes it clear that her prime objective is to win her husband over to Christ, both for his eternal benefit and also for their mutual blessing. The way she is to embark on this task is to "be submissive to" her husband, even those who "do not believe the word" (3:1).

Careful attention to behavior is the first emphasis. Earnest new believers find it hard to serve when their unbelieving spouses don't want to hear about Christ. Yet they must learn the art of practicing quietness instead of picking quarrels and learning cooperation rather than loving confrontation. Christianity should be highly visible, but not horribly vocal.

Careful attention to beauty is the second emphasis. Unbelieving men will probably love Peter's words here because they will save them thousands of dollars! Look at this: "Your beauty should not come from outward adornment, such as braided hair and the wearing of gold jewelry and fine clothes" (3:3). There is no reason to assume that Peter was opposed to feminine beauty but he certainly had no time for Christian women whose beauty was exclusively external. His principle here is to seek an expressive character, not expensive clothes; an inner attitude, not outer adornment.

Careful attention to bravery is the third emphasis. Using the illustration of Sarah who, "obeyed Abraham" and did "not give way to fear" (3:6) presumably when he required her to do things that would normally produce panic, Peter draws attention to the fact that many women in difficult marriages will need to be courageous and consistent if they are to achieve the greatest imaginable good for the one they love. If over a period of time, pagan husbands see a change of behavior that is positive, and a new beauty that is not just cosmetic, and sheer bravery that they know deep down in their hearts is superior to their own, there is a real possibility that new marriages will result as new men are born.

There is, however, another factor. Peter says that this kind of wife's behavior "is of great worth in God's sight" (3:4). This is a similar word of encouragement to that which he gave the slaves. He goes on to say, "this is commendable before God" (2:20). The Lord loves us all equally but perhaps He has a special place in his heart for this kind of wife and those kinds of slaves! Therefore, a good way to evaluate a marriage is perhaps to ask the question, "Is our marriage commending itself to God?" This kind of marriage is part of the call to "live such good lives among the pagans that, though they accuse you of doing wrong, they may see your good deeds and glorify God on the day he visits [you]" (2:12). Good Christian marriages have great worth in God's sight and great value in pagan society.

13

LOVING LIFE
1 Peter 3:8–12

A considerable body of theological opinion believes that the quote from Psalm 34 found in First Peter 3:10–12 was either adapted as a Christian hymn in the first century or became part of the primitive catechism. Either way, it is a beautiful passage of Scripture and the early believers memorized it so it might become an integral part of their thinking.

The theme of the passage is "loving life." There are different ways of looking at life. We can detest it, tolerate it or absolutely love it. We should ask ourselves about what needs to be built into our days so that we can feel, before God, that they are "good days." I think there are three things that we can draw from this passage that contribute greatly to our experience of the good life.

The Place of Belief

What we believe is fundamental to the lives we live. Many people seem to think it doesn't matter what you believe just as long as you believe it. Others require only sincerity of belief. But the world is full of sincere people who can admit they were sincerely wrong! The first thing that must be present is our belief in the existence of the Lord. Some believe that God is and the rest believe that God isn't, but everybody believes something! Those who believe that God exists find in Him the focal point, center and fundamental basis of existence. Those who believe that God does not exist must find a substitute center and basis of existence.

Peter built into his life a belief that the Lord is real. Not only that, he understood some specific things about the Lord. For example, he wrote "The eyes of the Lord are on the righteous and his ears are attentive to their prayer, but the face of the Lord is against those who do evil" (3:12). There are things that God is for and there are things that God is against. How does Peter know this? Because God has revealed Himself in His Word. He revealed in the ancient psalm that He is the God of reality and the God of righteousness. What we believe about God being the essence of righteousness and, consequently, anything opposite of Him being the essence of wrongness, will determine the whole of our lives. When right and wrong, good and evil are defined in terms of Him, in the midst of a society that has chosen to believe He does not exist and made their own standards, the uniqueness of Christian thought and behavior is obvious.

God is also the God of relationships, as is shown by His choice of the name Jehovah (translated "Lord"). Jehovah is the name that God chose to reveal Himself as a God who desires personal, intimate and deep relationships with people. This is one of the most magnificent things about divine revelation. God is not an impersonal force, a theological concept, the unmoved mover or the uncaused cause. He is one who freely chooses to introduce Himself to people so that they might live in an intimate relationship with Him—what the Bible calls "knowing" Him. "To know Him is to love Him" becomes much more than a hackneyed phrase reserved for eulogies when we apply it to Jehovah. And to love Him is to obey Him by living life His way.

There are also our beliefs about the experiences of life. Peter is quite straightforward about life. He says it's tough, hard and difficult. But despite all that, Peter tells us we should love it. Peter is a firm believer that God has given us all things richly to enjoy. It's interesting to notice that Peter, in quoting King David, aligns himself with the king who believed that life should be good and loved. But the writer of Ecclesiastes, who had similar opportunities and experiences to those of King David, came to an exactly opposite conclusion. In contrast to David's "I love life," he wrote, "I hated life." "Vanity of vanities" was his cynical summary of life. Everything is meaningless, he proclaimed! What we believe about life, whether it is to be enjoyed in relationship with God or endured in a maelstrom of meaninglessness, will affect every aspect of life.

We must also consider what we believe about the exercise of liberty. The Bible is replete with instructions and commands, and this passage has its fair share. If we accept that these are God's instructions to people, it is a reasonable assumption that God intends us to obey them. But in giving us the ability to obey, God gave us the liberty to disobey Him. A fundamental of human experience is that there is built in liberty. It is something that God has ordained. But this liberty, depending on what we believe about it, can be either an untold blessing or an unmitigated blight.

It is just as important to look into what we believe about liberty as it is for us to look into what we believe about everything else. For instance, when the Lord, through Peter, says, "Live in harmony with one another" (3:8), He knows perfectly well that some will produce more discord than harmony and be perfectly content with what they are doing. When He says, "be sympathetic" He knows some will choose not to be sympathetic. When He says, "be humble," He knows that some people will say, "That is the worst thing you can do! If you want to get ahead, you have to promote yourself!" In short, when the Bible gives us instructions, imperatives and commands it presupposes our freedom to obey or to disobey. But before the decision to obey or not, there has to be an ability to discern the options and consequences. God has given us that freedom too. What we believe about freedoms will have monumental impact on whether we live good days or bad.

The Place of Behavior

Behavior is inexplicably bound up in belief. Considerable research into human behavior patterns is being pursued at this time. Contemporary Christians need never fear honest, scientific discovery. But be clear about the "honest" part of that statement. Some "scientific" work is dishonest in the extreme because of its unfair, unwarranted presuppositions. Christians should be aware of this but equally aware of the folly of denying the helpful insights into human behavior being gained through secular research. Christian belief based on the ancient Book inspired by God and scientific discovery of the wonders of God's creation are both experiences of truth. The two should enrich each other.

One of the things that is rather obvious is that our behavior is clearly related to our convictions. What we believe deeply will make us feel deeply, which will lead to specific behaviors. For example, in verses 10 and 11, Peter quotes the psalmist who says that if we're going to enjoy life and "see good days" we must "turn from evil and do good." It's one thing to turn from evil and leave it at that, but the person who really believes that evil is evil should believe also that the opposite of evil should be embraced. In other words, there is real conviction about evil and good. It will not just be the avoiding of evil because it's nasty and might hurt us, but the "doing of good" to counter evil in others' lives.

Behavior is also related to circumstances. Some circumstances are basically agreeable. For example, verse 8 suggests a most agreeable situation where everybody is living in harmony with each other. Everybody is sympathetic, loves their brothers, compassionate and humble! Living in such circumstances would no doubt affect our behavior.

On the other hand, we may find ourselves in a situation where there are all kinds of evil and insults coming our way: tongues saying rotten things and lips spewing deceitful speech. There is much that is grossly unfair, unjust and inequitable, and we suffer because of it and are affected by it. Peter knows how circumstances can affect behavior, yet he insists there ought to be a dynamic in our lives attributable to the resurrection life of Christ that allows us to transcend circumstances rather than be consumed by them. How we handle our circumstances and what we do about our convictions determine how we behave. This decides whether or not we come up with a life we love and days that are good.

Behavior is also related to choices. When Peter says, "Finally" and then goes on for two more chapters, he is not betraying a common preacher's problem. *Finally* really means "in summary." He has given a lot of ideas and concepts to different groups but now he is summarizing it all for everyone. Everybody must now make some choices.

We must decide to live in harmony with one another. The word means literally to share a mind set. Some people think that when Christians live in harmony they are in agreement on every point. This is certainly incorrect! There is no hope of Christians coming to agreement on politics or economics, organizational structures, policies, objectives or strategies. We are not expected to do this. But we are required to develop the same mind set and share the same attitude. That's the key.

Remember that day that Peter decided the Lord Jesus needed an agent? He tried to demonstrate his own credentials for the post. But the Lord Jesus got rather upset and said, "Out of my sight, Satan" Now that's getting upset! Then Jesus added, "You do not have in mind the things of God, but the things of men" (Matt. 16:23). The word *mind* here is the same word *harmony* that Peter uses in First Peter 3:8, and I've got a feeling Peter may had some nasty vibes as he wrote it. He remembered when his mind set was way off and he had to make some decisions to get it in line. In the same way, he asks for Christian choices to be made. We must stop persuading each other to adopt our own mind-sets. We must decide that the attitude and mind-set of the Lord Jesus is what is right, and endeavor to bring our ways of looking at things in line with His. To develop the mind-set of Christ means submission, obedience, servanthood and sacrifice, all of which mean great big choices, every one of which is hard.

We must also choose to be "sympathetic." The English word *sympathetic* is simply a Greek word slightly polished. It means, literally, to suffer together. When we become aware of suffering, we are confronted with choices. When we see a man in the ditch, we may say, "tut tut" and keep going. Or, we might go over and look at him and say, "If he had taken proper precautions he wouldn't be in that fix" and keep going. Or, we can get down in his ditch, unload our little donkey and take the risk of caring. Being sympathetic requires a choice.

We must choose to "love as brothers." This means "to have a mutuality of concern." The beautiful thing about Christian brotherly love is that it puts the emphasis on our common Father. Scripture teaches that we are children of God through our new birth via the Holy Spirit who imparts the life of God to us. We are children of God by adoption. This means that God chose to bring us into His family and give us all the benefits that were not ours by right! This privilege is not ours alone. There are others who are sons and daughters of God, and if we accept that they enjoy God as we do, there is a very real possibility we might get around to enjoying each other. When the going gets tough, we tend to head for our own private little cave, building our own defenses and protecting ourselves from everybody and everything. This option is not available to Christians because we are required to build a familial relationship with each other.

We must choose to be compassionate. "Be compassionate" (3:8) is a translation of a fascinating Greek word. The second part of it is a word from which we get spleen, and is related to intestines. The Greeks talked about spleen, bowels and intestines the way we talk about guts. A very petite, feminine young girl was once introduced to me as a "gutsy little gal." The Greeks, like us, had the idea that your spleen, intestines and guts are related to courage. The Hebrews thought of "spleen" as determining concern and tenderheartedness. The first part of the word means good. So "to be compassionate" means to have some "good guts," "good feelings" and "good concern" for people. Frankly, that requires good choices!

We must choose to be "humble." That means be "lowly minded." Scripture tells us not to think of ourselves "more highly" than we ought to think. To be humble-minded means to have a realistic appraisal of ourselves before God. Some people are humble and proud of it. Their humility is sickening. They impose it upon you, attempting to impress you with it. They are so humble that they can go out through the door without opening it. They worm underneath and turn around to ensure that you saw it. On the other hand, there is a kind of arrogance that is equally intolerable.

To be lowly-minded is neither of these. It is to be totally realistic about who and what you are in the economy of God. And this requires a choice: will I believe what I want about myself or will I appraise myself by God's standards? Behavior is also related to calling. Peter says, from the depths of long hard experience, "Do not repay evil with evil or insult with insult, but with blessing" (3:9). Some might say, "That's the craziest thing I ever heard," while others settle for, "That's hard." Of course it's hard! Have you noticed how we think the next step after "that's hard" is "it can't be serious?" The important clause to notice is "to this you were called." We're really called, at this particular point, to choose not to react naturally but to respond supernaturally through the resource of the Holy Spirit within us. But, again, this requires making choices that we will only make if we believe that "to this [we] were called."

So we see how calling, choices, circumstances and convictions affect behavior. This, in turn, determines whether at the end of each day we say, "It was a good day, Lord. Thank you. Good night" or if we come to the end of another day with shame. It means we get up in the morning with a keen sense of anticipation and say, "Here comes another piece of life to love" or, "Here comes another piece of life to survive."

The frosting on the cake is "the blessing of God" which Peter says we "may inherit" (3:9). God is not committed to blessing sin, nor is He so naive that He puts His stamp of approval on our disobedience. His eyes are upon those who live rightly before Him. His ears are always open to the prayers of those who love Him and respond to Him. But make no mistake about it, His face is adamantly set against those who disobey. That being the case we recognize that the blessing of God is not something that we presume upon, neither is it something that we assume is ours by rights. The blessing of God, the stamp of divine approval, comes only on lives of which He approves.

The word *blessing* (*eulogia*) is the word from which we get *eulogy* and means, literally, to speak well of. Sometimes in a eulogy we speak so well of people after they are gone, attendees wonder if they've gone to the wrong funeral. A real eulogy, a real blessing, a real speaking well of is the product of thinking highly about someone. To bless somebody is to think so highly of them that you speak well of them and you pronounce good upon them. The blessing of God does this for us and ensures "good days." It ensures a life we love because belief and behavior bring delight to Him and that means joy for us.

14

WHAT REALLY MATTERS
1 Peter 3:13–16

In the Marines, we were required to whitewash our coal buckets. To me, it was the ultimate in futility but I had to do it anyway. One day I asked an officer why it was necessary for us to do this. He replied, "We are training you to do what you're told because one day your life may depend on your instantaneous obedience. If you get into the habit of arguing about everything you are told to do, you may find your head will be shot off while you debate an order."

This is not an attempt to encourage the enforcing of stupidity, but a reminder that the way we act when dangerous times come is usually determined by the things that have already been built into our lives. When the difficulty arrives, it is usually too late to try to build in the things that really matter.

A Matter of Confidence

Peter's question, "Who is going to harm you if you are eager to do good?" (3:13) is startling to say the least! The word *eager* in the Greek is the word from which we get *zealous* or *zealot*. He is not talking about doing good casually, but being sold on doing good. No doubt some of Peter's readers could answer this question from their own unpleasant experience. When they have gone out of their way to be neighborly and helpful, they have found that they were taken to the cleaners. So yes, at first sight it looks as if Peter has it all wrong. But he is not saying that if we try to be good, nobody will hurt us. His statement is much more profound than that. He is saying that if we are interested and committed to that which is really good, there is nobody that can get to us. Paul amplified Peter's thought when he wrote that such hurtful things as "trouble, hardship, persecution, famine, nakedness, danger or sword" cannot "separate us from the love of God." In fact, he added, "in all these things we are more than conquerors" (Rom. 8:35, 37). Both Paul and Peter teach that those people who are eager to do good are aware of the real good that God is working in their lives and, as a result, they are secure in Him.

Although Christians in the Western world sometimes talk about being persecuted by government officials or laws they don't like, it is doubtful if they should use the persecution word when we think of our fellow believers in other countries who are fleeing from their homes with nothing but the clothes on their backs. Far from homeland and loved ones, destitute and homeless for no other reason that they love the Lord Jesus, many Christians in our world face tribulation, pain and loss. Many more ordinary folks just worry about death and dying, or even life itself. But firm confidence in God's eternal commitment does much to banish all these fears to such an extent that it is very difficult to find for a believer who believes what he believes to be easily moved. It is easy to shake somebody who doesn't know what he believes or doesn't have any grounds for confidence. But Peter's readers had built eternal confidence into their lives and were well prepared.

Then there is an external confidence. Peter says, "Even if you should suffer for what is right, you are blessed" (1 Pet. 3:14). There is a popular philosophy abroad in our society that has to do with pain and pleasure. The popular perception is that we have the right to escape every kind of pain and to embrace every kind of pleasure. At first sight, this appears sensible enough, but a little thought will expose it as a dangerous fallacy. If we say that anything goes so long as we escape pain and enjoy pleasure, then pain and pleasure become the only determining factors. On this basis, "right" is avoiding pain and enjoying pleasure and "wrong" is suffering and being unhappy. The Bible speaks very forcibly against this. Peter says you can suffer for doing right. This popular secular attitude can lead only to self absorbed living. The way that Peter presents produces people who for noble reasons and high motives are prepared to sacrifice, to share and to suffer. Their underlying confidence in life is beyond the immediate and their rewards beyond the obvious.

Internal confidence is another important factor. Peter's command, "In your hearts, set apart Christ as Lord" (3:15) is a simple but beautiful expression. When I was a boy of seven, a very strange thing happened to me one Sunday morning. I was sitting absolutely alone. I wasn't reading anything, nor was I talking to anybody. There was no influence upon me. Into my mind came the strangest thought. I jumped from my stool by the fire and to my mother's amazement and consternation said, "You and Daddy are Christians but I'm not!" My mother immediately sprang into action and read from the Book of Revelation, Christ's words, "Behold I stand at the door and knock, and if any man hear my voice and open the door I will come in" (see Rev. 3:20). She explained to me that Christ who died and rose again was outside my life. He was knocking on the door because He wanted to come in and it was up to me to decide whether I would open up my life to Him. If I did, He promised He would come in. On that day, I simply invited the Christ who died for me to come and live within me and He did. I reasoned that He is either a liar or the Truth, and convinced He wasn't a liar, I allowed Him to enter my life.

But Peter says more than that. Christ must be acknowledged as Lord in the heart. We must recognize who it is we've invited into our hearts. The heart is like a house and Christ can be treated as we treat visitors. We may ask Him onto the porch to clean it up so the neighbors will think all is well. When the kids come along, we get a little scared with the responsibility and invite Him into the nursery. Then years go by and we have trouble with the teenagers, so we get Him in the game room because we're not too sure what games they are playing. Marriage problems follow so we invite Him into the bedroom. To set Christ apart as Lord is to honor Him rather than to use Him. It means to give him the bunch of keys and ask Him to invade each area of the heart with His transforming presence. To rightly understand the entrance of Christ into the heart we must accept the enthronement of Christ in the heart. This leads to the enjoyment of Christ in the heart. If we decide to keep part of our hearts for ourselves, when the going gets tough, we will be totally responsible for it. If, on the other hand, we open up our lives to His control, when the going gets tough He will be in control. That's when we begin to enjoy Christ in the heart, and that's where the internal confidence comes from.

A Matter of Conviction

Confidence provokes inquiry. Peter says we must be ready for this and writes, "Always be prepared to give an answer to everyone who asks you to give the reason for the hope that you have" (3:15). When someone says, "Excuse me, you seem to be remarkably confident. Would you mind very much explaining to me why you're so confident?" we must be able to explain the dynamics of our confidence. As a pastor, I have often rejoiced to see people who are suffering, exhibiting such courage and confidence that they are besieged by inquiries. I have been even more delighted when they have been able to clearly articulate the convictions behind the courage. Note carefully that Peter says we should always be ready to answer anyone. That's a rather all inclusive "always" and "anyone!" This does not mean that you should always have an answer for any question, however it is asked, on every subject. Peter mercifully limits it to questions about the hope within us. This is a great relief and a great challenge because it means that while everyone is not called to preach or be an apologist, it does mean that all believers must know enough about their own experience to be able to explain it. This requires a solid conviction that comes from learning how to define the things we're talking about. Peter calls them "reasons" which will constitute a defense of a deeply held position. An intelligent conversation requires both participants to know what the other is talking about because both may be using the same terms, but interpreting them differently. Something more than unexplained quotes and naive testimony is required. This takes time, study and practice; all of which are amply repaid when we have the privilege of sharing our convictions.

The way our convictions are shared is very important. I like the way Peter says, "But do it with gentleness and respect" (3:15). That means we are going to have to project real concern and esteem for the people with whom we share. Serious questions must be treated with the seriousness they deserve. Many questions don't deserve a serious answer. There are always some snarky individuals who ask questions like, "Where did Cain get his wife from?" Sensing this is not coming from a serious concern, I usually answer, "I would tell you if I was Abel, (pun intended)!" or "I don't know. I wasn't invited to the wedding!" But when people come to you with genuine questions and concerns, show that you hold them in high regard by listening very intently and doing all you possibly can to help.

The way we deal with people must also show that we have high esteem for God. If we act as God's representative, we assume an awesome responsibility. Explaining eternal truths to people is a burden of gigantic proportions. Jill was training a bunch of kids to go out witnessing in a supermarket. She asked me to give them a little pep talk before they embarked on their enterprise. So I went and I said, "You're going to go out to talk to people about things that are important so be very careful because you're going to meddle with eternal souls." My wife had a little word with me afterwards. She said, "Thanks a lot. I've worked with these kids getting them all excited about it and you come in and frighten the living daylights out of them."

I was somewhat chastened, but sharing convictions about Christ is more than having an argument, winning a debate or making a point. It is an attempt to represent God and present His gospel so that people who are without hope might discover the hope you have and also have confidence and conviction in times of trouble. Confidence and conviction go hand in hand and must be cherished and nourished.

A Matter of Conscience

Peter adds, "keeping a clear conscience, so that those who speak maliciously against your good behavior in Christ may be ashamed of their slander" (3:16). This has been noted before, so we do not need to repeat it. When we try really hard to stand for the things of God we will meet opposition. Many accusations will be made about which, we can do nothing. But there is one thing we can and must do: we must maintain a clear conscience. I vividly remember the testimony of a young missionary. When she was in Bible college, she worked in a high fashion store and over the years she robbed her employer of thousands of dollars worth of goods. One day God got through to her about her gross inconsistency. She went to her classmates, the authorities in the school and to her employer and made a full confession. She also made a promise to repay the man every penny she had taken from him. She not only did that but, when she was through, she led him to Christ. Her sensational story was hardly normal missionary fare and I was interested in the reaction. Some people thought she should have not made such a confession, but she said, "Listen, when you've confessed it, you're forgiven. When you're forgiven, there is nothing to hide. When there is nothing to hide, there is nothing to fear, and when there is nothing to fear you're free."

The trouble with conscience is that we can starve it so it becomes weak. Or we can do what Paul told Timothy and "sear it with a hot iron," (1 Tim. 4:2) so that it loses all sensitivity. Conscience needs to be in touch all the time with the enlightening truth of God's Word. A clear conscience, quiet confidence and solid convictions arm the humblest servant of the Lord for the struggles that may well lie ahead in a turbulent world.

15

SUFFERING

1 Peter 3:17–22

We know that people suffer because of the evil actions of others and we are also aware that some people who suffer have spent their lives doing good. So it is not surprising that people react to suffering in a variety of ways. Some have decided that there cannot possibly be a God because of all the suffering in the world, while others, who may not wish to deny His existence, certainly question His apparent impotence to check the turmoil or His mystifying acceptance of it. And, of course, one of the most common arguments for the "non-existence of God" is summarized in the aphorism, "If God is good, He is not great. If God is great, He is not good." Many who believe there is a God have become very angry with Him when suffering has come their way. So suffering is a highly volatile subject.

Yet Peter strikes a new note when he says, "It is better, if it is God's will, to suffer for doing good than for doing evil" (3:17). To suggest the possibility, as Peter does, that, "It is God's will that we suffer," is to introduce a powerful factor in our understanding of the mystery of suffering. We need to listen carefully to what the Scriptures say on the subject. Let's start with the sufferings of Christ.

Insight into the Sufferings of Christ

Christians don't understand many aspects of suffering but they do believe that God sent His only begotten Son to die on the cross where He suffered beyond our comprehension. So while we may wonder why God does not appear more active in our own suffering we do know that God identified deeply with humanity through His suffering. Furthermore, Christians, in identifying with the suffering Christ, know that they can hardly expect to be exempt from suffering themselves.

The sufferings of Christ were foreordained

Peter speaks of the prophets' desire to understand what the Spirit meant when "he predicted the sufferings of Christ and the glories that would follow" (1:11). In other words, the Old Testament predicts that the Messiah would suffer. Therefore, Peter concludes that the sufferings of Christ were not accidental and they were not explicable in terms of sociological concerns. They were not simply the result of human antagonisms or even the result of a good man suffering because He was surrounded by evil men. The sufferings and death of Christ, foreordained by God, was far from being God's plan coming unglued. The sufferings were God's plan coming to fruition. Before man was created, God knew exactly that the whole plan He had for the human race was going to be centered on His Son, our Lord, who would save a fallen world through suffering. Nothing makes this clearer than the brilliant biblical phrase that described him as "the Lamb that was slain from the creation of the world" (Rev. 13:8).

The sufferings of Christ were propitiatory

We are often aware that our sin hurts other people and in our wiser moments we recognize the damage we do to ourselves by sinning. But all sin is, first and foremost, sin against God. This is not adequately understood because some people seem to think they can sin and then forgive themselves, while others think that somebody else can forgive them. Suppose somebody got upset with me and punched me on the nose. While I am recovering from the blow I might mumble, "I forgive you." Then the attacker says, "You don't need to. I forgave myself." At that point, a third party would hopefully intervene and say, "Listen, you two, don't argue about it. Neither of you needs to forgive anybody. I forgive you both." This is ludicrous, of course! A third party couldn't forgive somebody for punching me on the nose, and somebody who punches me on the nose couldn't forgive himself either! Only the punchee can forgive the puncher! The Bible puts this in perspective with the question, "Who can forgive sins but God alone?"(Mark 2:7).

At this point we might be tempted to think, "Well God is God and He can do anything so why doesn't He just forgive our sins, give us a clean sheet and let us get on with our lives?" As attractive as this may sound to some, it betrays an inadequate understanding of who God is. He is holy and righteous so sin is an affront to His holiness. His righteousness demands sin must be judged. For Him NOT to judge sin would be a denial of justice and righteousness. To fail to offer grace, love, mercy and forgiveness would be contrary to His character. But in the cross of Jesus, He wonderfully combines both and so on the authority of Scripture we can and must proclaim that He allowed His Son to bear the judgment against sin thus satisfying divine justice, and leaving God perfectly free in love, grace and mercy to forgive sin.

The sufferings of Christ were substitutionary

Peter in his effort to clearly explain Christ's suffering wrote, "Christ died for sins, once for all, the righteous for the unrighteous, to bring you to God" (3:18). Christ was perfectly righteous before God, so there was no thought of Him dying for His own sin. He died on behalf of those who were not right with God. Not all Christians believe the same thing about the ones for whom Christ died. Some say "the elect" and others believe He died for the "unrighteous" or as Paul wrote, "we are convinced that one died for all, and therefore all died" (2 Cor. 5:14). At first read, this may suggest a universalist understanding of the cross whereby everybody eventually is forgiven. But Paul certainly did not imply that when he carefully added "that those who live should no longer live for themselves." In other words the death of Christ is efficacious for the sins of the whole world (all died) but not all will receive the gift of grace. "Those who live" will "live for him who died for them and was raised again" (2 Cor. 5:15).

The sufferings of Christ are conclusive

Peter writes, "Christ died for sins once for all" (3:18). The author of Hebrews made a number of similar statements such as "When this priest (that is, Christ) had offered for all time one sacrifice for sins, he sat down at the right hand of God. . . . by one sacrifice he has made perfect forever those who are being made holy" (Heb. 10:12, 14). Both the writer to the Hebrews and Peter set the sufferings of Christ in sharp contrast to other religious systems that require on-going sacrifices. They were thinking of the ancient Jewish sacrificial system, and possibly some of the pagan systems. Even some aspects of contemporary religion promote the idea that sacrifices for sin must continue, but this is a gross misunderstanding. When Christ died for sins, He did it once and for all. There is no necessity for any other sacrifice. His death was total satisfaction for all the sins of all people of all time and under all circumstances.

The sufferings of Christ were reconciliatory

This definitive statement further teaches that Christ died for sins to "bring you to God" (3:18). God made man in the first place so that man might know Him, love Him, serve Him and enjoy Him forever. But if we ask the average man and woman, "Do you know God? Do you love God? Do you enjoy God? Do you serve God?" they may struggle to an-swer these questions. This clearly indicates the alienation between God and man. Even if it were not clearly shown in human experience, it is unequivocally stated in Scripture that "your sins have separated between you and your God" (see Isa. 59:2). Therefore one of the greatest needs in the world is for God and man to be brought back to each other. Attempts to do this from our side of the gulf won't work because we don't have the materials or the inclination to get back to Him. Our only hope then is for God to take the initiative, work from His side to us and reconcile us to Himself. On the cross, Christ becomes a bridge across the great gulf between God and man. Through His sufferings, He makes it possible for mankind, repentantly, to come through Him, over the gulf into His presence to be warmly welcomed by a reconciling and a forgiving God.

The sufferings of Christ were extraordinary

When Peter wrote, "He was put to death in the body" (3:18), he used a brutal word that meant He was executed. Christ died in the most ignominious way a man could die. Everything that human ingenuity had been able to invent down through the long, sad history of human perversion had found its ultimate in the crucifixion.

Of all the deaths that Christ could have died, crucifixion was the worst. Maybe God not only wanted to identify with our suffering and our sin, but He wanted to do it at a depth deeper than any we had ever known. Maybe He wanted to suffer more than we could ever suffer in order to prove His unspeakable love for us.

But this leads us to the next statement that is somewhat difficult to understand. He was executed in the body but "made alive by [or in] the Spirit" (3:18). The word *Spirit* is capitalized meaning "the Holy Spirit," but it could just as accurately mean "the human spirit." Nobody knows conclusively, but I want to suggest that Peter is speaking of the human spirit of Christ in contrast to the body that suffered such brutal execution. Christ's death was terrible but temporary because He was executed in the body and immediately made alive in His spirit. For three days and nights, He moved in the nether regions. We can't be dogmatic about this because we don't know the details, but it would appear that Peter is saying that the Lord Jesus, quickened in spirit, "went and preached to the spirits in prison" (3:19). Speculations about the identity of these "spirits in prison" abound and dogmatism on the subject may be premature. Some have used this statement as a basis for believing that after the unconverted die they get another chance to be converted. This idea should not be encouraged for a number of reasons, not least of which is the word translated as *preach*. One Greek word for *preach* means to proclaim the gospel or to evangelize while another word means to declare or to make an announcement. Peter uses the latter and apparently means that Christ went into the regions "under the earth" and made a declaration to the forces of death and darkness that He is greater because He lives in the power of an endless life. Later, He was to rise from the dead to the Father's right hand, but already He shows after His apparent defeat that He is Victor. Bottom line? In order for the believer to understand suffering, it must be viewed through the prism of the sufferings of Christ.

Identification with the sufferings of Christ

Peter, on one occasion, said that he found some of the things Paul had written rather hard to understand (see 2 Pet. 3:16).

I'd like to know what Paul thought about the next piece of Peter's work! Peter's thoughts start bouncing off each other like balls on a pool table. They collide with one another and promptly head in new directions. Try to follow his train of thought as he starts talking about our suffering. That triggers his thinking about the suffering of Christ. Next, he talks about Jesus' death but he can't talk about that without thinking of Him being "quickened in spirit." This leads to what He did when He was quickened in spirit as He declared His victory to the spirits. Those spirits were in their present state because of the rebellion round about the time of Noah, so he detours to Noah and talks about the flood. The flood reminds him of water and water suggests baptism which, of course, speaks of Christians identifying with a suffering Christ. It's a relentless logic if you can follow it!

It is doubtful if there is a better illustration of God's dealings with man than the story of Noah. The moral order of our universe, with which we all must agree, requires that wrong should be punished and right should be rewarded. This order originated with God, so the inevitability of judgment follows hard on the heels of the sin of man. So we read that God looked down on the earth and was appalled with man's condition. He said, "I am grieved that I have made them" and immediately began to speak of judgment (see Gen. 6:5–7).

But God also exhibits grace and patience. Justice demands sin must be judged but grace reaches out to those who are sinning. Even as He announced the judgment of water, He instructed Noah to build an ark—the means of salvation. And as the ark was being built, God tolerated human sin for years, waiting patiently to show His grace and presumably, to give people more time to repent. The story of the flood is for Peter an *antitypos* of baptism—a symbol. It was an answer coming from a good conscience.

We might ask, "If baptism is the answer, what is the question?" I would suggest it is the question of God to man: "How do you hope to be reconciled to me?" And the answer in dramatic symbolism is, "by identifying with the crucified and risen Son through whom my sins were forgiven!"

Involvement in the Sufferings of Christ

In the same way that those who voluntarily identify with earthquake victims suffering from typhoid might succumb to the disease themselves, so can we understand how those who identify with the suffering Savior can become involved in His suffering.

Christians must expect to suffer, first of all, because of antagonism to Christ. Many people don't like Jesus. They don't like what He represents so they don't like His representatives either. They may get along fine with you if you "keep your mouth shut" and refrain from "stuffing Christianity down their throats," but once identified with Him there is no way to avoid being associated with His many unpopular positions and catching some of the antagonism that comes with those positions. We also suffer because we take stands against evil. I'm afraid many Christians have made their name for what they are against rather than what they favor. While we must be fundamentally positive and identify with what Christ is for, this also means we are against what He is against. That's when the fur begins to fly! Many people don't mind Christians being religious in a corner, but standing against evil involves stepping on toes!

In Washington recently, a "pro-choice" marcher carried a sign saying, "Keep your nasty morality off my body." She was saying, "I do it my way, you do it your way, but don't try and put your way on me because if you do I will take you on." Christians have a long tradition of taking a stand against evil, and when they do, somebody suffers and often it is the Christian.

Christians sometimes fall into sin themselves and suffer for their own stupidity. I am no fan of the devil but I do get upset when I hear the devil being blamed for Christian stupidity. This thinking is as inadequate as that of Flip Wilson, the former comedian, who popularized the punch line, "The devil made me do it." The devil can't make us do anything we don't agree to do. The Holy Spirit will empower our will, but if we decide to follow temptation, to do what is wrong and contravene God's law, there is no exemption from consequences. Suffering for spiritual stupidity and stubbornness is to be expected.

Christians also suffer because we are part of a fallen world. All of creation is groaning, creaking and longing for the day when everything will be redeemed and made anew. All kinds of crazy and cruel things are happening and we're not in an airtight capsule in the middle. We're part of it and we'll suffer with it.

Sometimes Christians suffer because it is the will of God that they should. Peter tells us on a number of occasions in this epistle that suffering is allowed by God to prove that our faith is genuine. One day the devil had a word with the Lord about Job. "What have you been doing?" said the Lord.

"I've been running to and fro having a look at your people."

"What do you think of them?"

"I don't like them!"

"Well, have you considered my servant Job?"

"Oh, Job, he is a faithful man, but look what you have given him. He's got everything! But take it all away and then see if he remains true to you."

God said, "Alright."

Calamity fell, Job suffered, and his faith didn't falter! Sometimes God will allow calamity to come to see where our faith lies. Not only did Job display his faith so powerfully, but he also glorified God by his steadfast commitment to Him—even through utter deprivation and constant encouragement from friends and family to "curse God and die."

Satan returned to the board room of hell knowing that he had been beaten by a pathetic man who was sitting on a garbage heap, scratching his open sores with pieces of pot. But this same man was also resting his tired body and aching heart in the merciful hands of an ultimately triumphant God. Christians in all ages have had the same opportunity to live for His glory through suffering when the going gets tough!

16

TAKING UP THE CROSS
1 Peter 4:1–6

The Lord Jesus told His disciples during their training, "Anyone who does not take his cross and follow me is not worthy of me" (Matt. 10:38). The disciples knew what it meant in their society to take up a cross. Execution by crucifixion was a dreadful fact of life in those days. The unfortunate victim being executed in this way was required to carry the cross beam on his shoulders, through the crowded, narrow streets of Jerusalem, on the way to the place where they would die. Information regarding name, family, home and crimes was nailed to the cross. It was a matter of great shame—an experience of terrible trauma. But the disciples, at the time, had little awareness of the connection between taking up the cross and being worthy of their master. In fact, Jesus hadn't even told them about the reality of His own cross.

The Appreciation of the Cross as Experienced by Peter

Simon Peter's brother, Andrew, having been introduced to Jesus as "the lamb of God who takes away the sin of the world" (John 1:29), promptly found his brother and told him, "We have found the Messiah" (1:41). The next day, Andrew and his brother went looking for Jesus who, upon seeing Simon, said, "You are Simon, son of John. You will be called Cephas (which, when translated, is Peter)" (1:42).

Peter was no doubt moved, mystified and intrigued by what Jesus said and when specifically called by Jesus to a life of discipleship promptly involved himself in following the Messiah.

As time went by, however, it became obvious to Peter that the Messiah was either losing His nerve or didn't understand His role. When Jesus announced to His disciples that He was going to be rejected and killed by the leadership of Israel but would rise again, Peter took him aside and began to rebuke him. "Never, Lord!" he said. "This shall never happen to you" (Matt. 16:22). Peter rejected any concept of the cross. It had no place in his perception of the Messiah's role.

It is not uncommon for people to have their own ideas of "Messiah" or the "Lord" or "God." Some manufacture their own Messiah and create their own Christ. Maybe it's a politician who promises what they want or a charismatic figure who tells them what they want to hear. Maybe it's a mover and shaker who promises to rectify all real and perceived ills. They accept these but flatly reject any concept of the crucified Christ. They are happy to have a Christ who fits into their preconceptions; a Messiah who organizes things the way they want them to be organized. But they would take their stand with Peter against a Messiah who starts talking about a cross and a resurrection. They welcome a

Christ who will come as an additive to their lives and sweeten the pot, making everything good, better and great. But a Christ on a cross is totally repugnant to them. Like Peter, they won't let Christ have a cross. They certainly won't entertain any thought of taking up one of their own as Jesus stated they must.

Later on, when it became obvious that the Lord was going to the cross, Peter denied any connection with Him. He defected. But one day the risen Lord Jesus appeared, cooked breakfast for him and said, "Peter, I want to ask you a simple question. Do you love me?" Now that had to be a hard question for Peter to answer because Jesus was really asking. "Do you love the Christ that I am as opposed to the Christ you created to suit your own purposes?" There was no doubt that Jesus had died, and there was equally no doubt that he was no longer dead! So Jesus was proven correct—he was the Messiah, though One who would be a Savior through death and resurrection not through any methodology that Peter had preconceived. Peter finally began to understand the cross and the reality of who Jesus is.

As he embarked on his apostolic ministry on the Day of Pentecost, Peter proclaimed the stupendous fact that Jesus was crucified on the cross partly because of the sinfulness of man but basically according to "God's set purpose and foreknowledge" (Acts 2:23). Years later in his pastoral ministry, as exhibited in the epistles, he wrote, "Christ died for sins once for all, the righteous for the unrighteous, to bring you to God" (3:18).

Slowly but surely, Peter had come to a solid appreciation of the cross of Christ. We need to trace the steps of our understanding to ensure that we too rightly relate to the Christ of Calvary.

The Application of the Cross as Explained by Peter

The word "therefore" in this passage links what is gone with what is coming. It ties principle to practice. Some people love doctrine but are not interested in applying it. Others just want practice, as they can't be bothered with doctrine. The Bible doesn't encourage either position. It outlines principles, inserts a "therefore" and launches into the practical application. Peter, having shown how he has come to appreciate the cross, now begins to apply the cross to his own life.

Applying the cross to our attitudes, he says, "Therefore, since Christ suffered in his body, arm yourselves also with the same attitude, because he who has suffered in his body is done with sin" (4:1). When Christ went to the cross, He assumed our sin and the sin of all people, in all situations, under all circumstances and for all ages. He then accepted the wrath of God against our sin and assumed, personally, the penalty of our sin. Having been utterly sinless, Christ became the personification of sin, the focal point of judgment and in Himself, the satisfactory propitiation for our sin. Jesus had nothing to do with sin before He came into the world. He tolerated a sinful environment and identified with sinful people while He was here and on the cross, He became sin for us. His experience of sin built into a remorseless, excruciating crescendo until, with a triumphant cry, He died for sin. At that moment, He was through with sin forever. It ought to be rather obvious that we who claim the merits of His death agree with His attitude toward sin and show it by saying that we wish to be done with it too. That means applying the cross to our attitudes. One of the contemporary attitudes toward sin is to call it by other names. Perhaps the "products of genetic imbalance," "the "result of environmental considerations" or "parental abuse." Some call it "an alternative lifestyle." We've got a plethora of substitute names for sin.

This is not to imply that many of the things going on in our world aren't alternative lifestyles. They are certainly choices or alternatives, but they are wrong choices and poor alternatives. Neither do we believe that environments and genetic considerations don't have a bearing on our lives. They do. But we must insist that while environment and heredity and family situations all produce certain inclinations and propensities toward sin, sinners decide to sin in the end. There may be all kinds of forces, all kinds of opportunities and all kinds of circumstances, but none of them can make us sin. In the final analysis, sin is a choice.

One of the first things we do, therefore, is to start calling sin, sin. Then we apply the cross to our attitude toward sin by developing a new attitude. Instead of excusing and condoning sin, we say it is incompatible with Christian conviction and therefore, choose to be through with it. There is much more to dealing with sin, but this is what Peter explains at this point. Recently a young pastor told me, "For many years I have been working as a social worker involving myself in many difficult situations. But I was limited in what I could say and do. Now that I am a pastor, I can open the Scriptures, apply biblical principles, sit down with people and help them work through their problems, including facing their sins. After a few months in the pastorate, I've seen more lives changed than in my many years as a social worker." This is definitely not a put-down of social work, but we accept that at the root of most of our problems are fundamentally sinful, selfish choices, and that the only antidote to those choices is a cross on our attitudes.

It's also critical to apply the cross to our ambitions. Peter continues, "As a result, he does not live the rest of his earthly life for evil human desires, but rather for the will of God" (4:2). Peter talks about "the rest of [our] earthly life" with particular reference to our ambitions. It is quite possible that our ambitions for the rest of life are fundamentally selfish. That being the case, we will be primarily interested in being comfortable, popular, making a profit, being exempt from pain and guaranteeing our own pleasure. These ambitions are all rooted in "me" and "mine" and "my." The problem with these human desires is that they can easily rule God out and that's when they become sinful.

There is an alternative position. We can say something like, "Lord, I fully realize that you have a plan for my life but my plan and your plan are in tension. My ambition, if I am perfectly honest, is to do what I want to do, and I would love your endorsement on my choices despite the fact that they are contrary to your choices. But I know it cannot work so I must apply a cross to my ambitions. And I remember that a cross is an 'I' ruled out."

The cross was not designed as an 18-karat gold ornament, or as a Christian symbol in religious places. It was intended for dying and that means dying, among other things, to the determination to go my own way. It means coming to the Gethsemane position of "Not my will, but yours be done" (Luke 22:42). This doesn't mean that we cease to be ambitious, but rather we are ambitious for what God wants.

I talked with a delightful well-trained young couple recently. He has a master's in education and she is an English teacher. They were very happy. Everything in life was coming together for them and then it suddenly dawned on them that perhaps they ought to explore what God wanted to do with their lives. They arrived at a startling conclusion. Of all things, God wanted them to teach English! What's startling about that? He wanted them to teach English in Chungking, China. So they are in the process of packing their bags, getting their visas, going behind the bamboo curtain, and seeking to be a presence for Christ in that new environment. They are ambitious for one thing only—the will of God.

We must apply the cross to our activities. Peter's description of the pagan life is graphic and his rejection of it is unequivocal. He writes, "You have spent enough time in the past doing what the pagans choose to do—living in debauchery, lust, drunkenness, orgies, carousing and detestable idolatry" (4:3). Pagan life involved all kinds of iniquity, impurity and idolatry. The word *detestable* here implies an activity that even the Roman Empire wouldn't tolerate.

The Christians to whom Peter writes were not fourth- and fifth-generation believers who were getting increasingly bored with each generation. They were fresh, newly converted pagans. They had all been up to their necks in a pagan lifestyle that had picked up such momentum it was carrying over into their Christian activities. They were prone to accept what even Rome declared unacceptable. Peter calls them to put a cross on these activities; these relics from an old life that contradicts with the new. The key, of course, is the phrase "doing what pagans choose to do." If pagans can choose to do things, converted pagans can choose not to do them. This is applying the cross. Not only terribly bad things have to be dealt with either. In my life, some very good and beautiful things have had a cross put on them too. Many years ago, when I was in my early twenties, I sang in a championship choir in Kendal, England. We practiced on Tuesday nights—the only night I had free. At that time, I was studying, preaching and working, so the Greenside Choir was my relaxation and hobby. I loved it! However, I began to feel decidedly uneasy about it and one day sensed that I ought to resign. I went to the director of the choir, explained, and she said, "Just tell me why, Stuart, why?"

I said, "I'm terribly sorry, but I can't. It has something to do with a Christian conviction that even I do not understand. You just have to believe me. This is no reflection on you." So I resigned, reluctantly, but knowing that in some way God was saying, "Put a cross on that activity."

The following day somebody asked me, "Stuart, what do you do on Tuesday nights?"

I replied, "I resigned from the Greenside Choir last night so my Tuesdays are free. It's the only night of the week that is free."

He said, "Good. A group of us have been praying that you would come to our town each Tuesday and teach the Bible to a small group of earnest people." So I did! About the third week of the study, an elderly lady became a believer. A week or two later, she died and I've often thought about the cross on my choir. Sometimes it comes down hard on the beautiful as well as the unthinkable.

Applying the cross to our associations is also important. Peter appears to speak from personal experience as he adds, "They think it strange that you do not plunge with them into the same flood of dissipation, and they heap abuse on you" (4:4). The people we used to associate with in all kinds of activities that were contrary to Christ will understandably get very upset with us if we pull out. They don't mind us being Christians as long as we continue in "the flood of dissipation." In fact, they will be most tolerant. They'll say things like, "That's neat! That's great! We're glad for you. You're into Jesus and we're into joking. This salvation bit makes you feel good and we feel better because we're on a diet with plenty of roughage. Different strokes, different folks." But when we find it necessary to say, "I'm sorry, deal me out. I'm sorry but I'm through. This is wrong for me now," things can change dramatically. The tolerance and camaraderie will likely dissipate into thin air. And, as Peter says, they may begin to heap abuse on you. I'm certainly not advocating evangelical isolation. Yet, there has to be a very clear-cut differentiation in the believer's life between his Christianity and his involvement in ambitions, attitudes, activities and associations that, in themselves, are contrary to Christ. Christ died for sin and is done with it. We died in Him, so we're done with it too. The cross has been applied and this is not once and for all—it's an ongoing experience.

The Appeal of the Cross as Expressed by Peter

Those who heap abuse on believers "will have to give account to him who is ready to judge the living and the dead" (4:5). Everybody is going to appear in the court of the judge. The One who will sit in the court as our Judge is the One who hung on the cross as our Jesus. There will be four categories of people standing before this Judge to give an account of their lives. There are those who will be alive when Christ calls for the great final judgment, and those who will already be dead. Peter calls them "the living and the dead" here. The living and the dead are then divided into two categories. Some who will be alive when He comes will also be spiritually alive; others will be spiritually dead. Some will be already dead but alive in Christ and some will be both physically dead and spiritually dead on Judgment day. So let's recap: At Judgment, there will be (1) living living and (2) dead living. There will be (3) living dead and (4) dead dead.

This is what will happen. The Judge will bring everything into account. The living and dead who are alive in Christ because they appreciated the cross and applied it to their lives, were forgiven and became disciples, will be told to enter into the joy of the Lord. The living and dead who are dead to Christ because they rejected the cross, manufactured their own messiah, created their own Christ and have absolutely no antidote for their sin, will be told by Judge Jesus, "Depart from me. I never knew you." The cross is the central factor in the coming judgment and disciples who recognize its majestic significance also demonstrate their understanding of its ongoing relevance by taking up their cross daily and following Christ.

17

LIVING NEAR THE END
1 Peter 4:7–11

T he end of all things is near," said the Apostle Peter as he contemplated Nero's bizarre behavior, the persecution looming on the horizon and the probability that he himself would not survive much longer. As he looked at his particular circumstances he had a tremendous sense that time was limited. But there was also something else on his mind.

Christian Belief Concerning "The End"

There is a fundamental principle in Scripture which, simply stated, says, "In the beginning, God created the heavens and the earth and in the end God will destroy the heavens and the earth." As surely as God, through His creative word, brought into existence the things that exist, so God, through His irrefutable command, will terminate all the things He brought into being. God, the initiator and the sustainer of all things, is also the terminator of all things. The Bible teaches an end to human history brought about by divine intervention.

Peter, as a Jew, had been taught from the Old Testament about something called "the day of the Lord." The people of Israel quite rightly believed that they were God's chosen people. They recognized that they had failed Him on many occasions, and had suffered much through their captivities. But even in the darkest hour, God, through His prophets, always had a message of hope for them. It was a hope that one day Israel would be what she was intended to be. The day of the Lord would come!

Israel also believed that the surrounding nations were heathen. They believed that the heathen quite rightly deserved the judgment of God. The "day of the Lord," as the Jewish people understood it in Old Testament times, therefore would be the day of Israel's vindication; a day of judgment for all those nations. Most saw it as a great cataclysmic event.

Peter thoroughly believed this as did the other disciples of our Lord Jesus. They were not able, therefore, to appreciate the heartbeat of the Master as they saw Him grieving over Jerusalem, and saying, "Oh, Jerusalem, Jerusalem . . . your house is left to you desolate" (Luke 13:34–35). And His disciples obviously didn't want to listen as He predicted awful things for Jerusalem.

They were too excited to be in the big city. They came from Galilee and were rather like kids from the country visiting New York for the first time and staring wide-eyed at the Empire State Building. As they excitedly shouted, "Look at these buildings! We don't have anything like that in Galilee," the Lord Jesus said, "There won't be one stone left standing on another in this city."

The disciples were puzzled and later came to Him quietly and said, "Master, Master, tell us when will this happen to Jerusalem, and when will be the time of your coming and when will be the end of the age?" (see Mark 13:1–4). Notice they asked three intertwined questions. This reveals to us that the disciples understood that "the day of the Lord" would incorporate the coming of Christ in glory.

They also assumed that if Jerusalem was going to be destroyed, it would be when God terminated all things, because, as far as they were concerned, if Jerusalem was destroyed then that was the end of everything. The Lord Jesus did not unravel these three ideas but He did show them that there will be a climactic, cataclysmic intervention of God in human affairs that will terminate history, and that this will take place at the glorious appearing and revelation of His Son, our Lord Jesus Christ. The only question remaining in the minds of the disciples was related to the timing of it.

As Peter stood up to preach on the day of Pentecost, he explained that the "end times" were beginning—that at that particular moment of history, the last days were dawning! How long the last days would last, however, remained a mystery locked up in the mind of God. Furthermore, Peter in his second epistle gives more details about the end of the world. He tells us that the heavens and earth will dissolve with fervent heat under God's direction. The same God who made all things is reserving these things for judgment and He, having initiated, will then terminate all things.

Everybody knows perfectly well that one of the over-riding concerns of the statesmen of our day and age is the threat of the unleashing of nuclear warfare. When nuclear arsenals belonged mainly to super powers, something called M.A.D. or "Mutually Assured Destruction" kept a nuclear holocaust at bay. But now nations known as rogue states and groups that are not even nations seek to seize control of nuclear weaponry. Add to this the dire warnings of climatic experts concerning global warming (although many people deny its existence) and the ongoing pollution of the atmosphere and there is plenty for secular man to worry about! Two thousand years after Peter announced "The end of all things is near" we seem to have arrived at this precarious position. The only thing is, we don't know how near. There is another aspect that must not be overlooked. None of us knows how near the end is as far as the termination of our individual lives. One day in Hong Kong I forgot, momentarily, that the traffic travels on the left side of the road. I stepped in front of a vehicle going at a tremendous speed and I can guarantee that it didn't miss me by more than an inch. Suddenly it dawned on me that I had been less than an inch from eternity. In this sense, the end is always near. It is never more than one breath away. Now, of course, this kind of topic can get people paranoid in a hurry. To be clear, Peter is not interested in producing paranoia. He is interested in producing living that is consistent with "the end."

Christian Behavior Considering "The End"

Peter gives a list of seven things that should characterize "end time" living. First, keep a cool head. Peter writing, "Be clear minded and self controlled" might sound strange coming from someone who has just announced that the end is imminent. But Peter insists that Christians don't panic. We must pray and pray properly so we can hold things together between their ears. How do we pray in panic situations? The best person to answer that is Peter himself. The Lord Jesus told the disciples to be witnesses unto Him but the authorities forbade them to do it. They went ahead anyway, were thrown in jail, threatened, beaten and let go. They promptly went back to their church fellowship. When they returned, they said, "Don't panic! Let's pray." How they prayed is recorded in Acts 4. They started off their prayer with the words, "Sovereign Lord." In panic situations start off by reminding yourself who is in control. Remind yourself that God is the "Sovereign Lord, maker of heaven and earth and the sea and all that is under them." The Sovereign "Lord, having made all things, is not going to let anybody else destroy His creation. He is going to do it!

Then the disciples quoted the Bible—Psalm 2 to be precise. A cool head is necessary to remember what the Bible says and to apply it to the immediate situation. If we panic in difficult situations, the quality of our praying will suffer. Having cleared the ground by basing everything on God's Word and sovereignty, the disciples further prayed, "Lord, give your servants boldness so that they may witness effectively" (see Acts 4:24–29). Their prayer was not for survival, but revival. This really requires a cool head because panicky people usually tend to pray panicky prayers for personal protection.

Second, keep a steady balance. It's very easy to become unbalanced when we think of the end times. When Peter talked about the end of all time, I'm sure many said, "Oh come on. You don't really believe that, do you? Everything continues the way it has from the very beginning." People talk like that today. They say, "We've got problems, I'll admit. But we'll solve them. I mean things are difficult, no question about it, but we'll handle it."

One of the most eminent men in Wisconsin has a firm conviction that education holds the solution for everything. I've talked to him, I like him, but I don't buy his philosophy that education will solve everything. Neither education nor any other human effort will solve the problem we've got when God decides, "Enough is enough!" We can't handle that one, folks, so we must not stick our heads in the sand and hope it will go away. It won't.

Other folks become so excited about the whole concept of the end that they decide to drop out of school. They have tried every other excuse, but this is the biggie! No one could knock this. The Lord is coming again. Some people try to say God has called them to the ministry but they don't want to go to seminary or Bible school because the Lord is coming again.

Some people decide that they won't equip themselves for a career because the Lord is coming again. Every generation of Christians has believed that they are living in the last of the last days. And each generation was wrong! So by the law of averages there is a good chance that those who go overboard in their approach to living in the end times will need to be rescued from drowning in their enthusiasm by those whose approach was more balanced.

An astronaut bound for the moon was asked, "How will you get off the moon?"

He said, "We fire the rockets and we take off in our little module."

"But what happens if it doesn't fire?"

He said, "Then we're stuck."

"How long will your life support system last?"

"Six hours."

The reporter then asked, "May I ask you what you will do for the last six hours?"

"Sure," he said. "I'll work on the engine!"

When we believe the coming of the Lord is near, we continue what we are because we are in the habit of doing what He told us to do. We are to just maintain the balance of expectancy and anticipation of our full lives if we die before He comes. But if He comes first, that will be just fine too! The believer in tune with Him simply keeps on fixing the engine!

Third, we must keep a warm heart. "Above all, love each other deeply, because love covers over a multitude of sins" (4:8) is the next piece of instruction. The words "above all" mean that love is the supreme Christian virtue.

When I joined the Marines I was loaded up with a pile of equipment that I had no idea how to use. An instructor saw me under the pile and said, "Don't worry about all that. Just learn how to fit your belt on. Everything else fits on it. If your belt is not right, nothing is right." Christians who worry about all their spiritual equipment might find it helpful to make sure their belt—in this case, love—fits properly. Then other things will fit too.

The word translated *deeply* here describes a sprinter or a race horse stretching for the finish line. We are to stretch ourselves to love, to recognize the supremacy of love and to keep a warm heart.

I heard a story about an Englishman who came to work at one of the rubber plants in Akron, Ohio. His first Sunday in town, he went to the pastor and said, "I'm here for two years, I'm British, I'm a Christian and I want to serve in this church. Please put me to work!" The pastor introduced him to a few people and he quickly became one of the best known people in the fellowship. There was never a Sunday when he didn't eat lunch with a different family in the church, not because he invited himself but because they all wanted to know him. He believed, "If any man would have friends he must first show himself friendly!" If we wait for people to love us, we'll find that they are waiting too. So we must start stretching and reaching out lovingly—because the end is near.

Fourth, keep an open house. The next verse says "Offer hospitality to one another without grumbling" (1 Pet. 4:9). The word for hospitality is literally the love of strangers or the love of foreigners. The word *xenophobia*, which means "the fear of strangers," has found a place in our vocabulary. But *philoxenia*, "the love of strangers," needs to appear in Christian terminology. In the New Testament, hospitality without grumbling was particularly important. The church in those days didn't have a sanctuary, a Christian education wing, gyms, administration blocks or mortgages. They met in homes because that was all they had.

When the fellowship met on Sunday mornings that meant somebody had to be given to hospitality, preferably without grumbling because a sour face can affect a worship service. Not only that, traveling evangelists did not stay at the Hilton. They had a choice between Christian homes and flea-ridden inns of iniquity. In actual fact, the life and growth of the church was measurable in terms of the hospitable spirit of those early believers. In addition, when people were thrown out of their homes and ostracized by their families after becoming Christians, they could not live on the streets. Other Christians took them in. They took in freed slaves and women who had been left by their husbands. Hospitality was the stuff of which the early church was made.

One of the great delights of Christian living is to use our homes instead of just preserving them for ourselves. If they can be used for a weekly study or for the kids to come and play, that's great. Perhaps, more realistically, we should consider a special hospitality issue. Somebody who is deeply concerned about the abortion issue told me he was so glad that evangelicals were speaking out, but he added a word of warning: "Before you shout too much about stopping abortions, have you made provision for the little gals who are pregnant out of wedlock? If you're saying 'don't abort,' what are you saying to the girl whose mother and father have kicked her out and her boyfriend has split for the Sun Belt? What are you going to do with that little gal?" Then he said, "If you are not prepared to open your home and take that girl in for nine months, maybe you should mute your criticism of abortion!"

Be given to hospitality!

Fifth, keep a faithful attitude. Peter writes, "Each one should use whatever gift he has received to serve others, faithfully administering God's grace in its various forms" (4:10). We know about God's grace. He graciously saves those who don't deserve it. We know about His grace that gives different gifts to those He has saved. We also know that He gives these gifts so that they might be used for the benefit of all. We are the trustees of these gifts with the understanding that on the Day of the Lord, He will evaluate what we did with what He entrusted to us. His sole concern on that day will be "did we live faithfully?" As we consider the end of our days, we should ask ourselves one question: "Will He say to me, 'Well done, good and faithful servant?'"

Sixth, keep a pure message. There is a special privilege in hearing God's Word and a peculiar pleasure in doing God's will. However, we must never overlook the particular pressure to share the Word of God. Handled properly, the Word produces fruit abundantly in the lives of those who receive it. Peter's admonition, "If anyone speaks, he should do it as one speaking the very words of God" (4:11) is especially significant in light of this.

Seventh, keep a powerful witness. Christians following the servant example of the Master need constant reminders of the necessity of nurturing a servant spirit. When reminded that a servant uses "the strength God provides" so that "God may be praised," there is motivation enough. But when seen in the light of the end of all things, any other attitude would appear obscene.

18

HANDLING HARSH REALITIES
1 Peter 4:12–19

Secular society seems to suggest that we have the right to always be happy, comfortable and successful. But that isn't necessarily so! This idea is more fantasy than reality, and we show our maturity by not indulging in fantasy but by handling the reality. This is basically Peter's theme.

The Word of God is sometimes almost brutal in its realism. It talks about the things that matter and it addresses life as it really is. Let us approach this passage in order to ensure that we are in touch with reality as expressed by Scripture.

There is nothing unusual or strange about painful trials (see 4:12). We live in a world that is far from ideal. Anyone can list dozens of things that are wrong with this world. Many people are getting hurt and many are experiencing difficult times. In a fallen world, people do wrong things so they suffer wrong things. We must face the fact that in a sinful, fallen, less than ideal world, all kinds of painful things will happen.

We also need to realize that God permits these things to happen. As we saw earlier, we may suffer "if it is God's will" (3:17). God has graciously determined that His people should not be wafted off to heaven on a pink-edged cloud to sprout wings, polish halos and play harps. He ordained that His people should stay on earth and live realistically in the real world. And what is this real world? It is a world that has many glorious and beautiful aspects, but is riddled with desperately painful parts as well.

I was reminded of this recently in Rio de Janeiro, Brazil. Rio, one of my favorite places on the whole face of God's earth, is indescribably beautiful unless you start looking at the realities of it. Behind rows of luxury tourist hotels facing beautiful beaches and glorious views there is a very steep mountainside split by deep ravines. In these ravines live a hundred thousand people in filthy, crime infested poverty. The real Rio is not only Sugar Loaf Mountain at sunset and Copacabana on a warm fresh morning but also the homeless orphans and rickety shanty-towns on the hillsides. It is in this world of gross inequity and evil imbalance beset by pain and pleasure that God ordained His people to live.

There is nothing strange about having a tough time, as Peter says, and mature believers learn to profit from these things. Immature people are much more likely to react and resent the things that are happening to them even though similar things are happening to the whole of society.

Again, we must not think it is strange if we encounter fiery trials. They are some of the harsh realities of life, permitted by God, from which we can grow. "Why me?" is the oft-repeated cry of those whose lives are difficult and disappointing. The answer that we must speak carefully and tenderly is "because we are a fallen people living in a fallen world where God allows the consequences of fallenness to befall us but with something positive in mind."

There is nothing sentimental about the sufferings of Christ. Peter says, "Rejoice that you participate in the sufferings of Christ, so that you may be overjoyed when his glory is revealed" (4:13). Way back before human history it was determined by the Trinity that the Son should participate in this world's sufferings. He was born in poverty. As a child, He was a refugee. He had to work very hard and lived under a repressive political regime. His contemporaries misunderstood Him. In the end, He suffered the ignominy of being charged and found guilty when He was innocent. Christ chose to identify with a suffering world, not in a technical sense, but in an intensely practical way. There was nothing sweet and sentimental about His suffering and we should avoid all temptation to rob His sacrificial lifestyle and ultimate death of either's harshness and pain. If we fail to do this we might give ourselves a rationale for fantasy living because we have translated Christ's reality into a fantasy world.

There is also nothing surprising about being insulted. Christians are sometimes insulted because of their Christian stance. We shouldn't be surprised at this, even when we are frequently hurt by it. Peter's perspective is important. He said, "If you are insulted because of the name of Christ, you are blessed" (4:14). Christians should learn to be blessed when we are insulted. Let me explain why. Christ is an insult to man's pride. Man thinks he is all right—or at least not all bad! He knows he isn't perfect but fondly imagines he's pretty close. The general consensus could probably be summarized as this: man is not perfect but with a little attention, he is probably perfectible! But Christ is the anointed Messiah who, by His life, showed how desperately short of "perfect" we have fallen and how totally incapable of rectifying our spiritual condition we actually are. This concept is an insult to the average person, a blow to our pride and a challenge to our self-sufficiency. When Christ stretches out His arms and says, "You don't realize how much you need me, and you can't do it on your own. Let me help you. I'll do it for you," the person who thinks he can solve everything is insulted by Christ and he reacts by insulting the name of Christ. So we must never be surprised when people insult the name of Christ. We who proudly bear His name are simply catching some of the backwash.

There is nothing spiritual about suffering for wrongdoing. Peter says, "If you suffer, it should not be as a murderer or thief or any other kind of criminal, or even as a meddler" (4:15). Christians are rather superb at doing stupid things and then spiritualizing them—trying to get some glory out of them. Peter sticks a pin in this balloon immediately. If we engage in some illegal activity, there will be legal consequences. If we engage in immorality, there will be moral consequences. This is not hard to understand but we may be surprised that Peter bracketed meddling with the other more obvious misbehaviors. The Greek word *allotriepiskopos* translated as *meddler* is as long as it is uncommon. The first half has to do with other people's business. The second means to watch over. If you put it all together it means to watch over other people's affairs or to stick your nose into other people's business!

Christians may have a problem at this point. We live in a pluralistic society. Some well-meaning believers feel responsible for our society. For example, they watch television that they rarely, if ever, see what Christians would regard as normal, healthy situations. There is no doubt that some of what is portrayed does represent a major segment of society, but some Christians feel that either our values should be given at least equal time, or that only Christian values should be broadcast. Some have even decided to take up that fight. They monitor programs, threaten advertisers with boycotts and generally rattle the networks' cages! Whether or not this is the right approach is hotly debated, but what Peter says is relevant and non-debatable. If we stick our noses in somebody's business there is a good chance somebody will whop it! If they do, we should not get all spiritual about it. A simple law of life states that he who sticketh his nose might findeth a fist on the end of it. Therefore, we must, at all times, check to see if our activities are illegal, immoral or simply meddlesome. If they are, we must not spiritualize the tough consequences that we experience.

There is nothing shameful about being a Christian. Peter writes, "However, if you suffer as a Christian, do not be ashamed, but praise God that you bear that name" (4:16). Followers of Jesus were not originally called Christians. The term was first used in the city of Antioch where people were notorious for giving everybody nicknames. So when disciples in their city began to follow Christ, they were given the less-than-complimentary name "Christians" (Christ followers). Believers accepted the term even though it was designed to be an insult and the designation stuck! Two thousand years later, the term Christian has lost much of its original meaning. Now it can mean little more than to be part of a certain culture or to adhere to certain ill-defined moral standards. It is even used as a means of differentiating from other major religions. But Christianity stands or falls on Christ. If Christ is not who He said He is, if Christ didn't do what He said He did, Christianity is a big hoax. If, on the other hand, Christ is who He said He is and He really did what Scripture claims He did, then Christianity is the only way to go and Christians have been smart enough to recognize it. So to be Christian still means to be identified with Christ as Lord and Savior. It is an identification that, by definition, sets the one bearing the name apart from secular society. This involves intellectual conviction that may create tensions in philosophical circles, moral standards that clash with secular norms, behavioral patterns that challenge and/or irritate those whose lifestyles are dramatically different and moral courage and spiritual faithfulness to take the convictions to their necessary conclusions. When that happens we must be ready to defend our position. In attempting to do so, we may lose a few arguments but if we stay on message—that is, if we tell people what Christ said and did and illustrate it from what we have personally experienced—we should be neither ashamed or embarrassed.

There are many shameful things about Christians though. Things our critics are far from reluctant to point out. Like everybody else, we are sometimes not very nice people. Church history is replete with skeleton-filled cupboards. We can't defend some of these things because they are indefensible. We must hang our heads in shame, admit to and regret our culpability. But we should never ever be reluctant to honor the name of the One we love and serve. And we should always praise God for the privilege!

There is nothing sacrosanct about the family of God. Some people have the idea that when we become Christians, we are placed in an airtight bubble and live in a state of spiritual weightlessness, removed and remote from all unpleasantness. But the tough, harsh reality is quite different! Peter knows this. He says, "For it is time for judgment to begin with the family of God; and if it begins with us, what will the outcome be for those who do not obey the gospel of God?" (4:17).

There is going to be judgment. We know, fundamentally, right must be rewarded and wrong must be punished. The surprising thing is that the judgment of God will begin with His people. Far from being in a position where realities hit everybody else and we escape, Christians can expect to be particularly vulnerable. What this means is, if the family of God doesn't do its job, God will not tolerate it, and church history proves this is true.

In the early days of Christianity the focal point was the Middle East. Today, there are lots of beautiful ruins throughout North Africa and Turkey and other regions of early church activities. In these ruins, you'll look long and hard for the Christian church. Later, Western Europe became a focal point so there you'll find superlative, beautiful, gorgeous cathedrals full of emptiness and tourists. From Europe, the center of activity moved to North America. Frankly, there are those who are saying that the momentum has moved from North America. Why? Because Christ has shown that if His own people will not accept responsibility and do not face up to accountability, if they think they are exempt from all difficulty, they are not living in reality. We are not sacrosanct, and the harsh reality is that judgment may come sooner than we think. The seven letters that Jesus dictated to the "angels" of the churches circling Ephesus make somber reading (see Rev. 2:1–3, 22).

There is nothing soft about God's will. The Bible does say that God's will is good and perfect and acceptable but it also says, "Those who suffer according to God's will should commit themselves to their faithful Creator" (4:19). So goodness and acceptability must not be regarded as the same as pleasant and enjoyable. Medicine is good, therapy can be perfect and surgery acceptable, but none are painless and pleasant.

A pro golfer friend of mine was doing so well that he was asked to go to the White House to speak of his success and show how it was related to his faith in Christ. Not long afterward, his game fell apart and he and his family suffered through hard times. When I asked him how he was getting along, he said, "This last year has been a total professional disaster but the most valuable year of my life because I have learned how to grow up."

Some of us need to face the fact that we may suffer according to God's will in order that we may be refined like gold in the fire. That hurts! It's one thing to know all this but another to know how to handle things when situations arise. But Peter gives us practical guidelines. First he wrote for us to be cheerful or, to quote him more accurately, "Rejoice that you participate in the sufferings of Christ" (4:13) and "do not be ashamed, but praise God" (4:16). Real praise and rejoicing come from deep within the heart, irrespective of the environment. That rejoicing can be expressed alone in a room or together in a congregation. It wells from the hearts of people who, confronting harsh realities, know what's going on and stand tall in their assurance.

The second instruction is to be content. Peter says "you are blessed" (4:14) if you are insulted for Christ. The word *blessed* is a technical, theological word that really means filled full and content. We don't have too many contented people around. There are many "if onlys" and lots of "why me's," but people who are content are rare. Some people are more docile and amenable than others but the contentment of which Peter speaks comes because "the Spirit of glory and of God rests on you" (4:14). It is the power of the Spirit of God that will enable us to stand firm and make us adequate. He is the source of contentment.

The third instruction is to be considerate. When talking about judgment and the Christian, Peter shows great sensitivity. He says, "If it begins with us, what will the outcome be for those who do not obey the gospel of God?" (4:17). One of the unpleasant things about believers is that we have such a nice time together that we can settle in glorious isolation and let the world go by. But the person who confronts the harsh reality of judgment is driven to compassionate action because the concerns of others are deeply etched on our conscience.

The fourth directive is we should "be committed to [our] faithful Creator" (4:19). Our Lord, on the cross, used the same word, "Into your hands I commit my spirit"

(Luke 23:46). At the moment of His greatest extremity, our Lord entrusted His well-being to His faithful Father who, of course proved magnificently faithful in raising Him from the dead. It is to the same faithful Father we commit ourselves to in the harshest of circumstances. We too will find him faithful and therein lies our confidence. The final instruction is to be consistent. Harsh realities produce hard attitudes and unhealthy reactions. But for the Christian, the call is to "continue to do good" (4:19). Hard times can easily lead to hardened hearts and may metastasize into bitterness and heartbreak. But a commitment to looking outward toward human need and setting one's heart to meet that need—to bless the needy rather than bemoan the circumstances—can militate against spiritual sclerosis and will leave the one doing the blessing spiritually healthy. Harsh realities are here to stay. They present the Christian with a plethora of choices all of which can be narrowed down to two: we can be hardened or we can be healthy.

19

TAKE ME TO YOUR LEADERS
1 Peter 5:1–4

Christians do not live out their Christianity on their own. Having identified with the Lord Jesus we become related to others who are identified with Him. This aspect of spiritual experience is of special significance during times of strain and stress because it enables believers to meet stress in a supportive group situation. It is also important that these groups have good leadership so that both the body and individuals might handle stress properly.

Peter has a lot to say concerning the church and the leaders of the church (or elders.). As a totally committed fisherman, it must have frustrated Peter to be required to teach about sheep, flocks and shepherds. But it is a fact that the Bible repeatedly used these familiar expressions to describe people in general and the church and her leaders in particular!

The People Are Like Sheep

Of all the animals the Lord could have chosen to describe people, he chose sheep. He could have said we were as brave as lions, as noble as horses or as beautiful as gazelles. But He didn't. This analogy is a singularly unflattering reference to our natural characteristics because, as mentioned previously, sheep are well known for their weakness and their waywardness. The Lord Jesus pointed out that sheep are particularly vulnerable when wild beasts come their way. Many of us might have little difficulty seeing that sheep is a valid expression describing our weakness because we have been ripped to shreds and often feel like sheep in the midst of wolves.

The Lord also talked about unscrupulous shepherds who were not interested in the well-being of sheep but were using the sheep instead of serving them. All of us can pinpoint situations where this has been our unhappy lot. Unfortunately, we have to admit that we are highly susceptible to the wild beasts and unscrupulous shepherds that abound in our society.

Sheep have a terrible tendency to behave in the most unrealistic and unhealthy ways. They love to wander, they have a nose for trouble and they follow without thinking. There is a natural tendency in our society for people to do things for no other reason than that everybody is doing it.

We have already noted that Peter said, "You were like sheep going astray, but now you have returned to the Shepherd and Overseer of your souls" (2:25). This is a clear echo of Isaiah 53:6 which reads, "We all, like sheep, have gone astray." Peter saw it firsthand as he traveled with the Master. On one occasion, the Lord took His disciples away for some relaxation time. To their intense frustration, a whole crowd of people came along. The Lord seemed to be concerned for them, but the disciples wanted to get rid of them. The word used to describe Christ's attitude was "that His stomach was tied in knots" and His concern came from His observation that they were "like sheep without a shepherd" (see Mark 6:31–34).

But Peter needed only to turn to his own experience for illustration! When the Lord Jesus quoted Zechariah 13:7—"I will strike the shepherd and the sheep of the pasture will be scattered"—to His disciples, He applied it to His impending death and the resulting flight of the disciples. Peter's response was predictable: "Even if I have to die with you I will never disown you" (see Matt. 26:31–35). When the Lord insisted, Peter would not accept it. So when Peter talks about wayward sheep, he's talking very personally because he knows the propensity of his own heart and the weak and wayward tendencies of his fellow sheep.

The Church Is Like a Flock

There is good news for all sheep because the Scriptures teach that if we are like sheep, then the church is like the flock. The Lord Jesus said, "I am the good shepherd; I know my sheep and my sheep know me . . . and there shall be one flock and one shepherd" (see John 10:14, 16). The intent of our Lord is to gather together out of every kindred and tongue and tribe and nation, from every social and economic and cultural background, people who will acknowledge Him as Shepherd and, therefore, will become one flock.

The Lord was often criticized because of His contact with some rather unsavory characters. His answer, in the form of a parable, was powerful and challenging: "Suppose one of you has a hundred sheep and loses one of them. Does he not leave the ninety-nine in the open country and go after the lost sheep until he finds it? On finding the lost sheep and bringing it home, he calls his friends and neighbors together and says, 'Rejoice with me I have found my lost sheep'" (see Luke 15:4–6). His uncompromising response to critics was that shepherds go after wayward, weak sheep to bring them into community where the shepherd can care for them.

So what is the church? It is a community of wayward, weak individuals who, like sheep, have gone astray. We know that the Good Shepherd gave His life for us, rose again and went after us personally, drawing us to Himself. In repentance, we came to Him, committed ourselves to Him and became members of the flock of God. Just like the fearful group of disciples who were told right from the beginning, "Do not be afraid, little flock" (12:32).

Hebrews 13 contains a wonderful benediction that reads, "May the God of peace, who through the blood of the eternal covenant brought back from the dead our Lord Jesus, that great Shepherd of the sheep, equip you with everything good for doing his will, and may he work in us what is pleasing to him, through Jesus Christ, to whom be glory for ever and ever, Amen" (13:20–21).

Presiding over the flock of redeemed, repentant, wayward, weak sheep is the Great Shepherd who has risen from the dead. His objective is to empower weak, wayward sheep so that they may be equipped to do the work of God as He works in them. The ministry of our Lord Jesus is initially to bring individuals to Himself. Having brought them to Himself, He places them into a massive corporate whole, the church, a body in which the sheer might of His resurrection is demonstrated as the church becomes a mighty, dynamic force for God in society. That this happened in the early days of the church can be seen in the way the original "little flock" became a mighty army, sweeping across the known world with the transforming message of the Shepherd.

The Bible presents the church as an invisible, universal and mystical body to which all "found" sheep belong. Equally clearly, it speaks of the body as being a local, tangible, visible group of people in a specific geographical location. This group is to be seen as God's special flock in which the Chief Shepherd is empowering the weak and wayward for works of service to the glory of God. This is a view not always appreciated by those who constitute a local assembly of believers.

These truths need to be strongly emphasized at the present time because it is not uncommon to find people who want to have a Shepherd but don't want anything to do with the flock. Whoever heard of a Shepherd who doesn't have a flock? Or worse, they want to be part of a flock but are not interested in a Shepherd.

The Elders Are Like Shepherds

When Peter wrote about "elders" his readers were familiar with the expression and the idea. No doubt the Jews among them were aware of what had happened to Moses. He had led a massive crowd of people into the wilderness and he was understandably tired of them. So Moses called together seventy elders and God assured him that the same spirit that rested on Moses, rested on every one of them. Multiple eldership was in operation—a principle of operation without which, the people of Israel could not have functioned in this tumultuous wilderness experience.

Peter's readers who came from a Gentile background influenced by Rome were no less familiar with elders! The Roman senate was comprised of people who were called the *Senex*, a word meaning old man. Incidentally, this is the word from which we get *senile* or *senator*, but I will make no further comment!

In Jerusalem, the Sanhedrin was also called the council of Elders. Peter, as we know, had his own special recollections of dealings with this body of august gentlemen. The synagogues that were established as a result of the dispersion of Jews who had lost their Temple was directed by elders!

In the light of prevailing principles of "elder" leadership, it is not surprising that the infant Christian churches were established with elders taking the lead. Some in our contemporary generation, particularly in the Western world, no longer looks up to older people. Attention is directed in the opposite direction as is evidenced by the emphasis on trying to look young. It almost seems as if we should not admit that we're getting older because old age is shunned or considered undesirable. Society seems to suggest that older people are becoming increasingly redundant and should be placed in a safe, comfortable situation where they can quietly fade away with minimal fuss and bother. I believe this is a dangerous trend away from a fundamental biblical principle that teaches us that as people get older, they amass experience that produces a mature, balanced outlook on life. Without in any way detracting from the obvious youthful virtues of enthusiasm, idealism and energy, care should be taken to preserve the mature participation in leadership which experience alone provides.

Two important functions of the elders are emphasized by Peter. The first is the shepherd function. He writes, "Be shepherds of God's flock that is under your care" (5:2). The Greek word for shepherd is also translated *pastor.* When we talk about a pastor, we're talking about a shepherd, and shepherding is an eldership responsibility.

Now Peter called himself "a fellow elder," classifying himself with others who shared the responsibly of leadership. No doubt, Peter's approach to shepherding was greatly influenced by the shepherding he received from the gracious Shepherd Himself. Having been carefully shepherded back into the fold after his dismal denial of Christ, Peter was himself appointed to be a shepherd.

Notice what he was required to do though. He was required to "feed lambs," "feed sheep" and "shepherd sheep" (see John 21:15–17). One of the mistakes made in many churches is that we do not differentiate between "feeding lambs" and "feeding sheep." If a lamb loses its mother, you pick it up, stick it under your arm, put a bottle of milk in the lamb's mouth and you feed the lamb. But you don't put a large woolly sheep under your arm and encourage the smelly old thing to suck on bottles. The adult sheep learns to feed itself! But that's not how many churches operate. The church must recognize that there are people who are weak and wayward and far from the Shepherd. To them, we present the Shepherd seeking to save them. When found by Him they become lambs who need some basic fundamental care. We need to spoon-feed them in the early days of spiritual growth. But as they grow into mature sheep we must teach them to feed themselves. The leadership, or shepherding, role in feeding must be clearly understood.

Shepherds of sheep must also be leading as well as feeding. Note how our Lord said, "My sheep listen to my voice; I know them and they follow me" (John 10:27). This is a strange concept to us because we have the idea of a flock of sheep being chased by a shepherd on a tractor shouting at a couple of sheep dogs. But in the Middle East, they still shepherd the way they did two thousand years ago. Little shepherd boys or girls, playing on flutes, wander over the barren wilderness and the sheep follow them nose to tail! Wherever the shepherd goes, they follow. One simple principle of the Christian church is that elders are leaders and leaders lead! The independent spirit that pervades our society has infiltrated the church, producing sheep who won't be bothered with flocks, members of flocks who won't follow shepherds and shepherds who have lost the nerve to lead! This is a gross caricature of the New Testament church, and both shepherds and sheep must share the blame.

Secondly, Peter talks about the overseer function as well. The Greek words *presbuteros* (an elder) and *episcopos* (an overseer) are used interchangeably. Both terms are talking about the same kind of people involved in the same sort of functions. Leadership, therefore, not only "shepherds" but "oversees."

Overseeing involved "caring for" as is seen in Peter's words. He says, "God's flock that is under your care" (5:2). God has ordained leadership in fellowships to care for sheep. Sheep are to gladly accept this care, and not identify it as an interference.

In our society, the wolves and unscrupulous shepherds are after sheep. Sheep, even though they've come to Christ, have not lost their sheepish tendencies! Therefore, in the flock of believers, we must have people who are giving oversight, caring for souls.

Overseers also have a watching out for aspect to their ministry. Paul and Barnabas, after they had established churches, decided to "go back and visit the brothers . . . and see how they are doing" (Acts 15:36). The word translated *visit* is a derivative of *episcopos*. In churches, large and small, it is all too easy for people never to share, genuinely, how they're doing, either because they don't want anyone to know or because nobody cares enough to find out!

The Hebrew epistle says, "See to it that no one misses the grace of God and that no bitter root grows up to cause trouble and defile many" (Heb. 12:15). This is relevant because the little expression "see to it" is also a derivative of *episcopos*. Overseers not only "watch out for" and "care for," but they also "see to it." They are the people who see to it that what needs to be done gets done in order that the church might be a church. It is clear from Scripture that while Christ is building his church, we are called to be part of this grand project by providing leadership that oversees and shepherds. In light of this we need to consider not only the function of leadership but also the frailties of leadership.

Elders are sheep just like the rest of the flock. All sheep have their problems but those in "leader sheep" carry both their own problems and other people's too. While they handle their own frailties they must care for the frailties of others. Peter points out some obvious frailties.

First, there are frailties in attitude. He said, "Be shepherds of God's flock . . . not because you must, but because you are willing" (5:2). It's like pulling teeth to get some people to exercise leadership in the church of Jesus Christ and sometimes those who do, lead with an attitude of, "If I don't do it nobody else will." That kind of grudging leadership produces grumbling "follower-ship." Leaders are called to lead with an attitude closer to enjoying it than enduring it.

Then there can be serious frailties in motivation. Why do we engage in leadership? Why do we shepherd? Why do we bother? Peter says, "Not greedy for money but eager to serve" (5:2) so evidently he was encountering problems with some whose motivation was closer to "loot" than "love."

Frailties in "style" regularly surface in the church. Peter's emphasis is on "not lording it over those entrusted to you . . . being examples" (5:3). Now there's a fine tension! Leaders have to lead, otherwise they are not leaders. But to some, that means demanding, dictating and domineering rather than encouraging, enabling and enthusing. Peter says leaders should be examples but he does not say examples of what! The example of the Good Shepherd is presumably what he had in mind.

Recently one of our elders, leading the congregation in prayer before I preached, said, "I hope Stuart has done his work this week. I hope he's been before God. I hope he's got a word from the Lord for us this morning. I hope he's prepared himself." It rejoiced my heart to be reminded that my leadership colleagues, knowing my frailties, don't criticize. They intercede for me before the throne that I might be a model, not a mogul. Leadership is determined by follower-ship. Hitler was a remarkable leader. He galvanized a defeated and dispirited Germany into a mighty nation, propagated a message that was embraced by millions and led Germany and Europe over a cliff. He was a world-class leader but where he led the people was disastrous.

This example and many others remind us that leadership requires qualities that some possess and others lack. But it also requires integrity, honesty, empathy and a love of people. Church leaders need to ask themselves three questions: "Is anyone following me? And if so, where am I leading them? And if not, why do I see myself as a leader?"

Leadership is never easy and demands much of those who bear its burden. As one oil company used to advertise on television, "You expect more from a leader." But if the elders, overseers, shepherds and leaders of the churches can keep in mind Peter's promise that "when the Chief Shepherd appears you will receive the crown of glory that will never fade away" (5:4), that should be motivation enough for them to serve faithfully and well.

20

THE MARKS OF MATURITY
1 Peter 5:5–14

Peter's epistle, written against the dark background of impending crisis, leaves the unmistakable impression that if believers respond to the information and instructions contained therein, they would be capable of behaving maturely and be equipped to handle tough situations. The closing section of the epistle contains a number of references to behavior patterns which I will call "marks of maturity."

Maturity and Authority

There is, in the economy of God, an absolute necessity for order. For there to be order, there must be authority that is recognized and respected. One of the marks of our maturity is the way we are prepared to accept authority and respond to it. Our secular society is suffering from a breakdown of authority. The unwillingness of people to accept authority is indicative of their immaturity because thinking people recognize that a society without authority will sooner or later self-destruct. The same applies to the church. We can identify spiritual maturity by the response, or lack of it, to authority in the fellowship of believers. Peter, therefore, tells young men, "Be submissive to those who are older" (5:5). And this, as we have seen, does not necessarily mean older in years, but may mean more mature in their Christian walk. Those who refuse to acknowledge authority show immaturity in their understanding of God's principles and lack of development in their spiritual and personal growth. These demand both discipline and a sense of responsibility.

Maturity and Humility

Peter goes on to say, "Clothe yourselves with humility toward one another, because, 'God opposes the proud but gives grace to the humble.' Humble yourselves, therefore, under God's mighty hand, that he may lift you up in due time" (5:5–6). Humility is frequently spoken about as if it is a precious grace that some have been blessed with and the rest of us greatly need. But Scripture points unerringly to the fact that humility is directly related to action on the part of a person rather than a gift that he or she passively inherits. Phrases such as "Clothe yourselves with humility" and "Humble yourselves," point to this with unmistakable clarity. Humility involves attitudes we adopt and actions we undertake. But what exactly do we mean by humility?

First of all, humility is based on a realistic assessment of yourself. Paul told the Romans, "Do not think of yourself more highly than you ought, but rather think of yourself with sober judgment, in accordance with the measure of faith God has given you" (Rom. 12:3). Paul draws a fine line in this injunction. Sober judgment or realistic self-evaluation is required and thinking more highly of oneself than we ought is obviously unacceptable. But thinking "more highly" than is appropriate is very different from thinking appropriately "highly" of oneself. This points to the fact that it is possible for people to think too lowly of themselves as well! So sober thinking or genuine humility says, "I'm a sinner saved by grace." Simply saying "I'm a sinner" is to do yourself an injustice—you are "saved by grace." That is a trophy of divine generosity—proclaim it and live it! Conversely to say, "I'm live by grace" and fail to admit being a sinner may ignore the ongoing inner propensity to sinfulness and suggest a triumphalist arrogance that is unseemly. But this is not an easy balance to maintain as a lady leaving our church on day discovered. She thanked the pastor for the sermon by saying it was the "best she'd ever heard." He, trying hard to be suitably humble in the presence of such adulation, replied, "Oh it was nothing to do with me, Madam. It was the Lord." To which she quickly retorted, "Oh it wasn't that good!" The pastor was right of course in attributing anything of eternal worth in the sermon to the gracious work of the indwelling Holy Spirit. But he was wrong to overlook the fact that he had worked hard, that he had exercised his gifts, that he had served God's purpose in proclaiming the truth and fulfilled his calling to "preach Christ" if only by grace! Christians ought to have a head start in the realistic self-assessment department. Those who have a low self-image, who feel utterly worthless, must not confuse that position with humility or spiritual maturity. Every human being has tremendous worth because we are created by God in His image.

It is something of an insult to the Lord Jesus to feel that we have no value when He emphatically demonstrated that we were worth dying for. Redeemed, created beings have been made heirs of God and joint heirs with Christ. They have the post of ambassador in His diplomatic corps, fully aware that the Lord said, "As the Father has sent me, I am sending you" (John 20:21). It is not humility to pretend to be less than God has created, redeemed, commissioned and equipped us to be.

To maintain the balance, however, we need to remember that apart from God's creation we would not exist and without His redemption we would be lost. Apart from His call, we would do nothing of eternal consequence. Genuinely humble people, knowing these things, avoid the ditch of unseemly arrogance on one side and the ditch of unwarranted self-denigration on the other, steering carefully up the middle of the road called humility. This is what we are called to do.

Secondly, humility is the result of rejected pride. Peter quotes Proverbs and says, "God opposes the proud but gives grace to the humble," (5:5) probably with great feelings reinforced by his own painful proof of the statement's truth. Peter's pride problem had been painfully exposed more than once as he walked with Jesus but not always in agreement or harmony. His public boasts of superior devotion and unbecoming statements of self-sufficiency were publicly shown to be hollow.

What then is pride? Pride is (1) to think grandly of our own capabilities apart from God, (2) to feel inordinately superior to others and (3) to reject what God says and to

decide to go our own way. Perhaps the most succinct statement of God's aversion to pride is found in the ancient Book
of Proverbs. It reads, "I hate pride and arrogance, evil behavior and perverse speech" (Prov. 8:13). The word used here
to describe God's action (opposes) is the word used for a
general getting all his armies lined up! In other words, God
sees the proud person and commits Himself to marshaling
His divine resources against that person to bring him down.
That sounds very cruel of God, but it isn't. He knows that
"pride goes before destruction, a haughty spirit before a fall"
(16:18). God commits Himself to bring the proud back to
earth with a bump, if necessary. But compared to the crash
and burn that often follows arrogant rejection of grace and
independent dismissal of divine direction, the "opposing" of
God is a "soft landing" much to be preferred.

Thirdly, humility is the result of resolute action. The
words translated "clothe yourselves with humility" mean,
literally, put on an apron. There is no question in my mind
that Peter is thinking of the day Jesus took off His outer garment, picked up an apron or a towel, put it on, took a bowl
of water to Peter and said, "You're first." And Peter said,
"You're not going to wash my feet" only to be overruled
and told that he didn't understand but would later (see John
13:2–10). At the time of writing his epistle, Peter under-
stands because the Lord Jesus had given him a very simple lesson in humility. Humility is being prepared to serve.
Pride is not being prepared to serve anybody, but expect-
ing to be served. Humility is taking off the trappings and
putting on the apron. Pride is totally immersing ourselves
in ourselves, wrapping ourselves in ostentatious garments

of self indulgence. Peter's words bear repeating, "Humble yourselves, therefore, under God's mighty hand, that he may lift you up" (5:6).

We rightly assume that Peter learned his pride lessons because of the shift in tone of this epistle from the brash boastful days of his burgeoning discipleship. Peter's experience is surely a huge encouragement to all of us who feel diminished by our own recognition of unseemly pride but are encouraged by the promise, "that he may lift you up in due time" (5:6). I began to learn the sting of God's rejection of pride and his promise of transformation from it many years ago as a young man.

The great American preacher, Donald G. Barnhouse, was preaching at the well-known Keswick Convention in northern England. I was in rather unwilling attendance. He began his sermon with a statement that riveted my attention and instilled in my heart a principle that reverberates to this day. It was a paraphrase of 1 Peter 5:5–6: "The way to up is down and the way to down is up." That is basically what Peter was saying and what I've been trying to explain.

Maturity and Anxiety

There are degrees of anxiety. Normal anxiety is necessary. If people were not concerned enough to provide food and shelter for themselves, many people would be cold and go hungry. Natural anxieties about safety, shelter and food are perfectly normal and totally necessary for survival. Then there is moderate anxiety. This is motivating. Some people whose jobs are absolutely secure, get paid whether they work or not. They know if they get fired they will be reinstated, so they don't produce. Others know if they don't produce they will be dismissed and there are plenty of people looking for jobs. So they work hard, even anxiously, making sure the boss can see what they're doing.

Now when the Bible says, "Cast all your anxiety on him because He cares for you" (5:7) it is talking about excessive anxiety that is enervating. Peter heard the Master speak about anxiety on the hills around Galilee. He remembered what He said about lilies being well dressed and birds being well fed because God cared for them. Peter had shown he was anxious about his position and recognition, and about what would happen if he left his family. He got upset, worried and uptight all the time. Nervous tension built up in him, bursting out in anger and frustration (see Matt. 6:25–34). But somewhere he arrived at a solid conclusion that his God was God and that God cared about him. He accepted that God promised to supply his needs and, therefore, while normal and moderate anxiety were necessary and healthy, extreme anxiety was out of order. That this was a conscious decision is shown by his use of the aorist tense meaning a radical once and for all decision to trust and not be afraid. This was a decision that would require constant reaffirmation.

Maturity and Sobriety

Peter's solemn words, "Be self-controlled and alert. Your enemy the devil prowls around like a roaring lion looking for someone to devour. Resist him, standing firm in the faith,

because you know that your brothers throughout the world
are undergoing the same kind of sufferings" (5:8–9) needed
to be treated with great seriousness. His sober assessment
of the situation in which many believers were living because
the enemy of souls, the devil, was on a rampage, was causing him pastoral concern because he envisioned the persecution spreading in the direction of those to whom he was
writing. Peter anticipated tremendous persecution and he
saw behind this persecution an enemy who was real and
dangerous. In the Western world, where the church knows
little about persecution, it is no coincidence that we don't
know much about the enemy of our souls either. But in recent months and during the last few years, militant terror-
ism has spread into the heart of major cities such as Paris,
London, New York and potentially to anywhere and everywhere else.

The Middle East has seen ancient cultures reduced to
smoldering ruins and ancient peoples uprooted from their
homes, businesses and churches. People living hitherto in
assumed safety and a corresponding casual approach to
devilish activity, have become more than a little alarmed
and more than a little aware of evil in its most naked and
visible forms; an evil that has shown up on their doorsteps.
Perhaps for the first time, Christians in the west are feeling
vulnerable and insecure.

To be self-controlled in this context means, at least,
don't panic! But more than that, it means to take careful
stock of the situation. "Stand firm in the faith" means know
what you believe about God and life, evil and grace, Jesus
and the Holy Spirit, salvation and ultimate glory. Put it all

together, and stand firmly on it. As for the devil, heed the advice of C.S. Lewis who pointed out the two extremes to which people tend to gravitate when the devil is the subject. Some become obsessed and practically paralyzed by him; they see him behind every beard and under every bed. Others ignore him or dismiss him from the realms of reality altogether. Lewis pointed out that either way, the devil wins and moves forward unmolested with his nefarious plans. Always remember that having done all in his infernal power to stop you from coming to Christ and failing, he can't get you back. But he will do all he can to stop you from growing and maturing. Sober assessments of spiritual vulnerability and spiritual forces are marks of spiritual maturity.

Maturity and Stability

"And the God of all grace, who called you to his eternal glory in Christ, after you have suffered a little while, will himself restore you and make you strong, firm and steadfast. To him be the power for ever and ever. Amen"

(5:10–11).

Once again Peter brings up the subject of suffering and again he talks about it as if it is a certainty rather than an unwelcome possibility. Presumably, approaching it this way leads to a more stable response to suffering when it arrives. But Peter does not concentrate on the suffering aspect this time but rather on the activity of God in the life of the suffering believer. And what gracious activity he outlines for us!

First, stability is predicated on the presence of the "God of all grace" (5:10). I love this expression even though it doesn't do justice to what Peter actually says. The word *all* here means many and varied types of grace. Every kind of grace for every kind of problem. There is nothing we will ever be called for that God does not have the right grace for us. I am not a practical person when it comes to fixing things but I do enjoy periodic visits to hardware stores. Wandering along rows and rows of ingenious pieces of equipment, I marvel at the variations of size, material, shape and purpose in which such common items as nails and screws are manufactured. There is a nail for every kind of hole and a screw for all conceivable fittings. God's store is like this. He has every kind of grace for every kind of situation!

Second, stability is found in "God's mighty hand" upon our lives (5:6). The Old Testament character Ezra is one of my heroes! He faced enormous odds and challenging situations, often with an understandable degree of trepidation, but he always came back to a fundamental belief that "the good hand of his God was on him" (Ezra 7:9). Ezra's consciousness that God's hand on his life was "good," married to Peter's understanding that God's hand is "mighty," paint a picture of the supporting, holding, protecting, empowering, nurturing, restraining, directing, and yes, stabilizing hand of the Lord being always ours.

Third, stability is found in the recognition of our calling to "Eternal glory in Christ" (5:10). Peter has talked much about being called and some of his teachings may have been a little hard for suffering people to accept. But there is one aspect of God's call that all of us can appreciate and anticipate. It is the promise that the consummation of our call to follow Jesus is "eternal glory." To know that when my temporal life has ended, I will embark on a new life with eternal dimensions, and then to recognize that this never ending state will indeed be "glorious," sweetens many a bitter cup of suffering and serves to make us "strong, firm and steadfast" as the God of all grace works in our lives.

This, Peter assures us, "is the true grace of God" and we are to "stand fast in it" (5:12).

People submitted to Christ's enabling have a tremendous sense of stability because they know they stand firm in the mighty hand of God and in the eternal call of God. Notice that God calls us to His eternal glory after suffering a little while! The two aspects of the call of God—to eternal glory through earthly suffering—must not be separated.

We maintain stability when the going gets tough by knowing that we'll finish up in glory having traveled a path of suffering. There is no resurrection Christ without a cross, in the same way there is no eternal glory without some degree of earthly suffering. Deathbed conversions are better than no conversion, but do give the impression that, sensing the ship is sinking, those who suddenly are concerned, bail out and get in God's lifeboat. This can be a gross misunderstanding of God's call. The call of God is not to live our own lives our own way and, at the last minute with our last breath, say whatever it takes to get Him to take us to eternal glory. The call of God involves earthly suffering because through it, we magnify His power to keep us and demonstrate His grace in our weakness. Earthly suffering, bravely borne, shows powerfully the reality of the living God. When it is over, we can lay down our weapons and enter into rest. This broad perspective provides the base upon which spiritual stability is built.

All these things are marks of maturity outlined by the apostle so that when the going gets tough, those of us exposed to the toughness will have developed the Christian caliber necessary to withstand until we see the glory of God.

PUBLICATIONS

Fort Washington, PA 19034

This book is published by CLC Publications, an outreach
of CLC Ministries International. The purpose of CLC is to
make evangelical Christian literature available to all nations
so that people may come to faith and maturity in the Lord
Jesus Christ. We hope this book has been life changing and
has enriched your walk with God through the work of the
Holy Spirit. If you would like to know more about CLC,
we invite you to visit our website:
www.clcusa.org

To know more about the remarkable story of the founding of
CLC International we encourage you to read

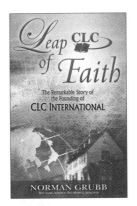

LEAP OF FAITH

Norman Grubb

Paperback
Size 5^1/$_4$ x 8, Pages 248
ISBN: 978-0-87508-650-7
ISBN (*e-book*): 978-1-61958-055-8